I wish I had had this book years ago, as I began to think through the whole dating thing. It's like having your very own mentor for relationships, who is for you, encourages you, doesn't judge you, who is honest but also challenging. *The Dating Dilemma* not only takes you through what the Bible says on dating, but it also answers the questions people can be ashamed to ask, in a way that is understandable and down to earth. Whether you have never dated, have dated lots of people, are about to get married, have been hurt time and time again, or just really let down by love, this book brings hope and excitement for wherever you are on your journey.
Esther Davenport, Soul Survivor

Rachel and André are the kind of people you would want to have a coffee with and talk about relationships. They are funny, unashamedly honest, deep and profoundly practical. If you are ready for a romance revolution where you live love, as well as have a love life, get this book – or take André and Rachel out for coffee.
Ian Henderson, The Message Trust and founder of nakedtruthproject.com

This book does an amazing job of unpacking some of the unhelpful myths that have taken root in the church, and gives a godly context and perspective for dating and relationships. It is packed with down-to-earth, practical and biblical teaching, providing both encouragement and challenge for its readers. If you're serious about following God in every area of your life and want to date and relate in a godly way, I urge you to buy and devour this book.
Mike Pilavachi, Soul Survivor

THE
DATING
DILEMMA

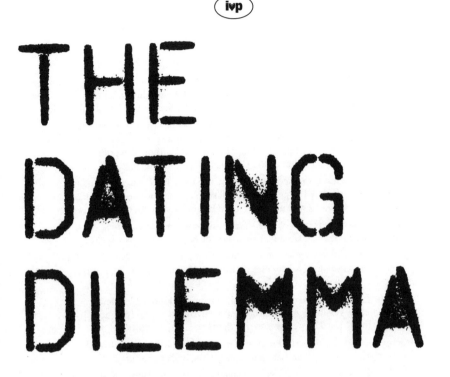

THE DATING DILEMMA

A ROMANCE REVOLUTION

RACHEL GARDNER & ANDRÉ ADEFOPE

www.relationshipdilemma.com

Relationship Dilemma @relationdilem

INTER-VARSITY PRESS
Norton Street, Nottingham NG7 3HR, England
Email: ivp@ivpbooks.com
Website: www.ivpbooks.com

First published 2013

British Library Cataloguing in Publication Data
A catalogue record for this book is available from the British Library.

ISBN: 978–1–84474–623–1
ePub: 978–1–78359–002–5
Mobi: 978–1–78359–003–2

Set in Dante 11.5/14pt
Typeset in Great Britain by CRB Associates, Potterhanworth, Lincolnshire
Printed in Great Britain by Ashford Colour Press Ltd, Gosport, Hampshire

Inter-Varsity Press publishes Christian books that are true to the Bible and that communicate the gospel, develop discipleship and strengthen the church for its mission in the world.

Inter-Varsity Press is closely linked with the Universities and Colleges Christian Fellowship, a student movement connecting Christian Unions in universities and colleges throughout Great Britain, and a member movement of the International Fellowship of Evangelical Students. Website: www.uccf.org.uk

Dat-ing: a stage in a person's life when they are preparing to actively pursue, are actively pursuing, or are in pre-marriage romantic relationships

Ro-mance: a feeling of excitement and mystery associated with love; an ardent emotional attachment or involvement between people

Rev-o-lu-tion: a forcible overthrow of a social order for a new system

How we came to write this book

This book has two beginnings.

One starts with a bottle blonde (Rachel) on a TV documentary series, challenging teenagers on the first ever Romance Academy to think deeply about their romantic and sexual relationships. The other begins with one of those teenagers from the series (André), all grown up and writing a master's degree dissertation about God's view on dating. We have put this together to produce a book.

But it's not just 'another' book on dating. At least, we don't want it to be.

Here's why we wrote this book, in our own words:

ANDRÉ: My thinking around relationships began nearly ten years ago when I wasn't a Christian. I was in high school, and, like most teenage lads, I wanted to get a girlfriend and have sex. Mainly because all my friends told me this was what I should do, and my hormones didn't want to disagree. In amongst all this confusion, a friend dragged me to a youth church service, and the talk was about sex. It challenged me to think about why God invented it, and how it could really bless or hurt me and those around me. It resonated deeply, so that night I committed to saving sex until marriage. A few weeks later I became a Christian. You're probably thinking that I did that in the wrong order, but I guess God has a good sense of humour.

That night God *instantly* and miraculously cured me of a porn addiction, and by his grace he has allowed me never to look at it since. However, God has *slowly* challenged my attitudes and approach to women and relationships over time. By getting into his Word, I have discovered that relationships are one of his ultimate gifts to us. A right relationship with him and others can fill that gap which my selfish desires and warped view of women never could. Along the way I've had a number of would-be girlfriends reject me, a failed relationship with a non-Christian, and for a while I even thought God was calling me to singleness (and no sex) for life! So for about six months I completely stopped looking for a relationship. Through all of this, God has been teaching me how to be selfless in my friendships, and honouring and intentional when I did date again. Eventually I asked Becca out, and we have been dating for over four years now.

I have made a lot of mistakes over the years, and I know it's not just me who struggles with approaching relationships God's way. I have seen so many Christians get hurt, and hurt others, out of selfishness, manipulation, or because they didn't want to, or know how to, seek God in their relationship. So when I studied at London School of Theology, God challenged me to write my dissertation on dating. (Who said romance is dead?!) But this wasn't about advice based on my experience, but about getting into the depths of God's Word to see if dating can be justified biblically, and if so, what it would look like. After I had finished, I gave a copy to my brilliant and wise friend Rachel. Over coffee she suggested that we write a book that took my academic research and infused it with well-thought-out practical advice. As you can tell, I said yes . . .

RACHEL: Relationships matter. Male or female, young or old, Christian or not, we all want to be happy, fulfilled and excited by the relationships we're in. For the past few years this has been *the* topic that I've talked about more than any other. Teenagers in the local schools where I do lessons call me the 'God/sex lady', which is a bit weird, but also great: they see that God has something to say about sex! I meet many young Christians who feel torn when it comes to handling their romantic relationships. On the one hand, they are ready to surrender everything to Jesus. But on the other hand, they are wrestling with emotions, urges and expectations that sometimes feel in direct conflict with what a Christian should face. More often than not, they bury their questions or ditch dating altogether, and then feel guilty about the relationships they're in or struggle to know whether this (good) relationship is *the one* to last a lifetime.

There are so many dating dilemmas that I really wanted to get my head round. Then André took me out for coffee. He had just finished his master's dissertation, in which he had written extensively on whether the Bible supports the idea of modern dating at all. He decided that it did – and I liked the sound of that!

We decided to turn his work into a book for Christians who want to build their romantic relationships in a godly way. I could think of no-one better than André to work with on this book because we have history! Back in 2005, I was involved in a BBC2 documentary series called *No Sex Please, We're Teenagers*, in which a bunch of North London teenagers were asked to be celibate for five months. André was the only Christian teen taking part in the programme, and it was quickly obvious that his commitment to doing relationships God's way ran deeper than a short course. The success of the TV series inspired my co-presenter Dan Burke and I to found the Romance Academy, and help other young people to benefit from approaching their relationships with 'God-goggles' on.

A book like this isn't for everyone. And even though we've put loads of thought, prayer and research into it, we won't have covered every dilemma. We're sorry about that. But we trust that, like us, you will appreciate being able to think through dating in a new way and look to building your significant relationships on strong foundations.

You never know where it might lead!

I want to say thank you to my family, who supported me emotionally and financially through my education. More importantly, thank you for showing me unconditional love and acceptance throughout my life, and for making me laugh every day. I will always be grateful.

Most of all, thank you to Becca, my fiancée, whose patience, grace, love towards others and passion for God constantly inspire me. We have been dating for over four years now, and it has shown me that relationships are worth the hard work. With God at the centre, they just get better and better. Thank you for all of your forgiveness, support and belief in me, and in us. I love you.

André

Jason
We're a team.
And I love every moment of loving you.

Rachel

We would like to say a huge thank-you to the IVP team, especially our wonderful editor Sam Parkinson for his passion for this topic, as well as his way with words.
It's been a real team effort!

CONTENTS

PREFACE

This book is *not* about being single.

And it's *not* about getting engaged or married.

It's about dating. We believe that when it's done well it could change your life!

But what if you've already gone out with an amazing Christian who you thought was 'the one', but it didn't work out? What if 'the-one-you're-seeing-right-now' doesn't love Jesus? What if there are 'no-suitable-dates' on the horizon? Should you wave goodbye to romance, or get out there and risk falling for 'the-*wrong*-one'?

Could there be a way for Christians to meet and mate that *doesn't* involve your pastor arranging your marriage, or your home group introducing polygamy? Is it possible to have godly, romantic relationships, even if they don't end in marriage?

It is.

We think it's highly likely that God won't tell you who you're going to marry. Not because he doesn't have a destiny for you, but because he wants you to use the mind and heart he's given you to make choices in line with his desires.

We have a hunch that he's OK with you getting to know someone romantically before choosing whether or not you want to marry them. Not because he thinks feelings are more important than faithfulness, but because he wants you to learn that outrageous selflessness and unquenchable love go hand in hand.

We think God can accept dating (with a few tweaks here and there) as a good way to learn some godly relationship skills. Not because he's obsessed with people hooking up, but because he's heartbroken about marriages breaking down. Not because he wants us to do 'whatever we feel like', but because, when dating is done badly, it can lead to casualties.

So here's a question we know is worth asking: Is God not just OK with dating, but also passionate about it? And if he is, shouldn't we find a way to date that God celebrates and which our society will think is revolutionary?

We think the answer is a resounding 'yes'. We're not turning around the way God sees romance, but the way *we* see it.

So buckle up, rev the engine and brace yourself.

Your love life could be about to get a whole lot more interesting!

Boy and girl meet.
Boy and girl fall in love.
Boys *just knows* girl is 'the one'.
Girl *just knows* boy is 'the one'.
So boy buys ring.
And girl says 'yes'.
They live happily ever after and never argue.
Just how God planned it.

Really?

INTRODUCTION:
THE ONE

Worst nightmare

It was 3am, and for the second night running I (Rachel) was sitting up in bed in a cold sweat. As I looked down at the sleeping figure of my husband of three months, I was gripped with a fear I could hardly voice. What if I had married the wrong guy? What if 'the one' I was destined to marry was still out there somewhere? What if I was now going to spend the rest of my life never knowing what life *should* have been like?

Jason rolled over and saw me sitting bolt upright in bed. 'You can't sleep?' he murmured groggily.

'Just got a lot on my mind,' I mumbled.

A few days later, I told Jason of my deep, dark thoughts.

'Don't worry about it, babe. Everyone thinks that at some point.'

'Do you think I might not be "the one" for you?' I asked, astounded.

He shrugged: 'Sure, sometimes. But then I remember that a more amazing thing than falling in love is growing in love. We're going to work at that for the rest of our lives.' And with a wink he was off to work.

Jason and I have been married for over ten years now, and whenever people ask us how we knew that we were right for each other, we tell them, 'We didn't know if we were each other's "one"; we just got married!' OK, so we loved each other, got on well together and shared our love for Jesus, but it's been the years since of getting to know each other and working hard at our relationship that have made us realize how great we are together. Most of the time!

And this reveals a dilemma we hear voiced in lots of different ways by lots of different Christians at the events and churches where we speak about relationships: 'How do I find "the one" God has for me?' (The other main question is: 'How much sex can we get away with when we're dating, before God says it's naughty?' But we'll come to that later!)

Both guys *and* girls ask us about finding 'the one'.

And with this question comes an assumption that God will engineer our love life. The logic goes: he loves us, he loves marriage, so he'll make sure we get the right person to date. Won't he?

There's an episode of the American comedy *Friends* that begins with Phoebe asking everyone if they believe in soulmates. Rachel is emphatic: 'I believe there is one perfect person for everyone. All we need to do is find them.' She works her way through many failed relationships, but in the last ever episode her hopes are realized, as we see her running off the plane and into the arms of long-term on-off love, Ross. It's one of the longest running love stories in a sitcom and confirms our belief that, in the end, we'll get what we've always longed for. If God loves us (which he does), and if he promises to give us the desires of our hearts (which he does), then it's obvious that he'll help us find 'the one'.

It's a story we hear time and again, but it's simply not a promise that God makes; it's not biblical.

Please don't throw this book down in disgust! We're not saying that God doesn't have a plan for your life or that he doesn't care about your hopes for finding love. Because he does! But we need to be careful that we don't translate that into some vague belief that God owes us a great romance, or even a husband or wife. Why? Because it can lead to all sorts of ungodly attitudes and behaviours, particularly when it comes to dating. How many people do you know who have been dumped because the person they were with had some fantastical notion about the perfect relationship God had waiting for them just round the next corner? How many people do you know who went too far sexually with someone they were dating, only to blame their ex, or God, for not keeping them pure? If we believe that God will one day swoop in, clean up the mess made by our bad dating choices, and present us with Mr or Miss Perfect, then we don't need to ask him to transform us.

We might find 'the one', but then feel totally unprepared for the reality of building a relationship with another person who is just as flawed as we are!

Perfect love

We often hear Christian couples talking about their relationships in super-spiritual ways: 'Looking back, we just knew'; 'God told me that the next person I saw would be my marriage partner'; 'My previous relationship had been a disaster, but this time it felt so easy – no arguments. It just felt right, so we knew God was in it.' This can convince us that we will know automatically who we need to marry.

Soon after I (André) became a Christian, I felt that God had chosen one of the girls at the church to be my future wife. I prayed really hard, and then, I thought, came the revelation that we would start dating in six months. Naturally, I praised God! But as you may have guessed, not only did I *not* go out with her; she went out with someone else. But it was OK, because around the same time I thought God was telling me that I had heard wrong, and that there was in fact another girl he had chosen to be 'the one'. But that relationship didn't work out either. So what was going on? God is a good God after all, and wanting to find someone is natural, so why was he not making it happen? Wasn't he supposed to make it easier for me?

Does this sound familiar to you?

Sometimes God does like to intervene with details of who someone should marry. We heard the story of a woman whose grandma told her that she would meet her husband in the next two months. So she ditched her current boyfriend, and met and married this new man. It has worked out well for her, but for every story like this there are hundreds, if not thousands, where deciding whether or not a hunch is God's guidance has been more difficult or totally disastrous. Martin and Amy both felt God had given them clear signs that they should be together, so they started dating, but it was all over in three months. Sally and Keith married after an intense whirlwind romance. It felt so good that it must have been from God. But years later, with very little in common and struggling even to sleep in the same bed, they wondered whether they really had heard from God.

Where does this leave 'the one' idea?

Once I (Rachel) had talked to Jason about my concerns about how we would ever know if we were each 'the one' destined by God for the other, we began to see how exciting our relationship could be. You see, if I thought Jason was mine by some cosmic design and then things went wrong, the only logical conclusion was that we were not destined for each other and we were missing out on God's best for us. Once we both realized that we had married each other not just for our own sake, but for each other's, we began to find ways to invest in each other and build our relationship.

I (André) came to understand that holding on to 'the one' belief robbed me of something. I was putting my faith in the *plan*, instead of the God who holds time and space in his hands. I was sitting back and waiting for things to happen, rather than drawing close to God and discerning what he wanted me to do next. It wasn't a girl that would make sense of my life, but a deepening relationship with God.

When it comes to God's plan for your life, we believe that the idea of 'the one' isn't good enough.

It doesn't help you if you are heartbroken and think your mistakes have robbed you of God's plan for your life. It doesn't help you if you are dating but waiting for a sign from God, instead of working on the relationship. It doesn't help you if you are married and struggling through difficult times. It doesn't help you if you are single and feel your life is on hold until you find your 'destined' someone.

God's plan for your life isn't dependent on your dating status, which means that your capacity to live life to the full isn't limited by it either. God can do anything in and through us, at any time and in any way! 'Now to him who by the power at work within us is able to accomplish abundantly far more than all we can ask or imagine, to him be glory in the church and in Christ Jesus to all generations, forever and ever. Amen' (Ephesians 3:20–21 NRSV).

It might seem harsh to hear this coming from the two of us; we've found the people we want to spend the rest of our lives with! Except it wasn't like that. Neither of us got a sign in the sky or a word from heaven or even a sense from God that we were about to meet the person we were meant to marry. Jason and I (Rachel) didn't even get on that well when we first met. Becca and I (André) didn't remotely fancy each other for years. We were just friends. So although we're not looking for someone to date, we understand the many pitfalls strewn across the path of anyone looking for love.

We're also not going to regale you with tales of our 'perfect' relationships. Firstly, because they're not perfect, and secondly, because sadly we've seen, time and again, how a focus on marriage as the happy ending Jesus will 'magic up' for us gets in the way of our thinking about how to date well.

This isn't a book of top tips on how to find the partner God has destined for you. It's biblical and practical wisdom on how to discover the life God has destined for you, and how to relate to those around you in a way that honours God. But there's no reason to think that won't include romance and dating.

Look at how God works with people in the Bible. We never see God waving his 'holiness wand' to make people's situations better. Instead, when they went through hard times, as well as good times, they had to learn to draw closer to God. That was the source of their hope and fulfilment. Not their wealth, significance or relationship status. Joseph, who was sold as a slave, falsely accused of rape and imprisoned, turned to God and grew in character. Eventually he rose to a position of power, saving thousands from starvation, and blessing his family and the people of God in the process! The apostle Paul was beaten, whipped, shipwrecked, imprisoned, stoned, and much more. But he got to spread the gospel, and thousands were saved.

A relationship with God doesn't remove us from the challenges and difficulties of life. The challenge is to seek God on our journey. Can we be real about where we're at, and open it all up to him? When we do, we find a shift in our destination, away from what we think we need to make us whole, towards wanting to be more like Jesus, whatever our circumstances.

So should we just give up on looking for love?

Not at all!

But our search needs to be surrendered to God.

Opened eyes

Maybe you're not expecting perfection in life or love. And maybe you're not expecting God to give you a message in a bottle about who you should date. You just want to find someone you could *possibly* consider getting married to. So what part do you see God playing in that? How do you handle the challenges and possible confusions thrown up by dating?

One friend recently told us of her less-than-ideal first date with a man she was hoping might be Mr Right, only to find that he 'turned up for the date with a tub of melted ice-cream in hand

and a tacky oil painting from Marbella of boats in a harbour as a gift, and proceeded to tell me "just to clear the air" that he categorically did not believe women should preach, and that he was a good date compared to some!'

A friend and I (André) once invited a couple of girls out to a fireworks display. The girls thought that a massive group of us were going, but we had 'forgotten' to tell them that it was a double date. I was pulling out all my best chat-up lines and turning on the charm, so naturally I was convinced that one of them liked me. The next day, just as I was about to ask her out, her boyfriend came up to me and introduced himself.

Awkward!

Relationship-status confusions, clumsy comments, feeling too shy to truly be yourself all seem to be part of the pre-marriage-relationship stage that we are left to navigate on our own. In researching this book, we've met people who feel really hopeful for their futures, as well as those who are hurt and confused by broken relationships. Wanting to know what God thinks about their relationships is a theme that runs through lots of these conversations. We've also come up against some pretty strange ideas about dating. We've met Christians who believe that any form of pre-marriage romantic relationship is dishonouring to God; Christians who have developed a nervous tic around checking wedding ring fingers; Christians so crippled by sexual sin that they believe they don't deserve a loving relationship; Christians who believe that their 'romantic-God' has their ideal guy/girl just waiting for them; some Christians who even believe that 'try-before-you-buy' (sex before marriage) is essential in order to establish compatibility.

There seems to be so much confusion around dating that often gets in the way of discerning God's guidance about our relationships.

The good news is that God *does* want to be involved in your pre-marriage relationships. He wants us to surrender every area of our lives to him, so that he can transform it for his glory. The question is: how? In rare instances, God might point out the person you're going to marry. And if he does, good stuff! But most of the time, he's more interested in who you're *becoming*, not just who you're dating. Throughout this book we are going to be exploring some incredible truths God has for you. If God helps you to grow in confidence around the opposite sex, or teaches you the keys to understanding commitment, he is guiding you towards any future relationship just as much as if he had told you your future spouse's name and address! Learning to be less self-centred in a dating relationship is one of the ways God can help you to become relationally intelligent and able to serve others – whether you marry them or not!

God knows that relationships aren't always easy. Beginning to share parts of your world with someone else can feel a bit uncomfortable at times. So he wants you to be prepared, emotionally, physically and spiritually.

Zack got married a few years ago. His marriage is everything he hoped it would be, but recently he told us how difficult the first year was. Nothing had prepared him for how much he was about to discover of his own flaws. Counselling has helped him come to terms with insecurities that had gone undetected or unchallenged throughout his life. But his one regret is that he waited until he was married before he looked at who he was and what he had to offer anyone in a relationship.

The 'perfect relationship' mantra might inadvertently make us think that, when our relationship hits hard times or doesn't always feel amazing, it's a sign that we aren't with 'the one' God has for us. We might even think that, if we're not convinced we want to marry someone ten minutes into the relationship, we shouldn't keep dating. A relationship you need to work at is no less a gift from God. A relationship that doesn't *begin* with a commitment to getting married any time soon is no less valuable in God's eyes. You might end up discovering a greater appreciation for each other that will grow into the deep love needed for a strong relationship. You'll discover how working through difficulties gives you an increased resilience and capacity for forgiveness. These are vital tools for building marriages that last. More importantly, if we date in a way that allows our character to grow in selflessness and maturity, then even if the relationship doesn't work out, it will honour God. Isn't that better than thoughtless dating or waiting for God to sort everything out?

So in all this uncertainty around romance, we think that it's probably time for a bit of honest talking about relationships, sex and, most specifically, dating.

To date or not to date

So let's start by unpacking what we think dating is. It won't always be the same as the wider culture's ideas about dating, but more of that later. First up, dating is not the most important thing. You might not feel ready or even interested in dating yet. You're not alone!

> It's not that I don't want a steady girlfriend or marriage. It's just that my life is so busy, I don't think I would have time for a relationship. If someone comes along, then great – but I'm not looking for it.
> (Phil)

> I genuinely don't want to settle down yet. I know that as a nice Christian girl I'm not supposed to say that, but I like being single.
> (Tracy)

For anyone who is interested in dating, it's about spending time with someone you're attracted to and you enjoy being with. For some people it's also about finding that connection.

> I'm an intuitive person; I trust my gut 90% of the time! So nothing gets me more excited than a spark; that instant and

mutual attraction to someone is amazing. Whilst I totally
believe it can develop over time, I don't think anyone can ignore
that chemical reaction – so it's definitely what I look for in a
potential date!
(Andrea)

We do believe that dating is about marriage potential to some
degree. Whether you're meeting over a milkshake, cuddling
through a movie or climbing Kilimanjaro together, dating has a
long-term focus: to see whether this relationship has what it
takes to go the distance. The moment you are sure that it doesn't,
it's probably time to stop being romantically involved. This is
not the same as only dating someone you are convinced you can
marry from the moment you clap eyes on them! The goal of
godly dating is Christian maturity and good marriage, not
marriage from the start or marriage at any cost.

I am happy to date a few girls. I don't have a problem with that.
It's just that if it becomes really obvious that we're not right
together, then I'm not about to keep something going just
because I can. There's no point. I want to get married, but not
just for the sake of it.
(Al)

But there's something else about dating that we should mention.
It's not biblical.

For this reason, some Christians don't date at all, or will only
consider marrying close friends, skipping the whole dating stage.
Mark believes that, on the whole, dating people you don't know
is 'overrated and filled with too many pitfalls. You're better off
going out with your mates.'

But before you think we've conned you into reading about
dating when we're going to say God hates it, we're not.

Dating isn't biblical in the same way that preaching with a
microphone, texting, recycling, or driving a car aren't biblical: it

didn't exist before the twentieth century. Dating is a contemporary practice that the church in the West has bought into. So if it's not in the Bible, should it be in our lives?

There have been voices in recent years calling for Christians to avoid any relationship that isn't destined to end in marriage. On the surface this sounds wise. As people who believe in the sacred covenant of marriage, we should avoid relationships that demand little in the way of commitment. But we think that tying yourself to a no-dating rule will pose more problems than it solves. Taken to an extreme, there are Christians who have felt an obligation to marry the first person they fancied, and were 'kind of dating', even if they said they weren't. In rejecting dating but still wanting to find someone to marry, we can find ourselves in a kind of no man's land before marriage, with no clear boundaries for what we can or can't expect from the other person in this new relationship. The Bible doesn't talk about the internet or globalization, and while these things carry the potential for incredible evil, Christians are constantly trying to transform them and use them for God's glory. So why can't we transform our Western dating culture, using the biblical principles for relationships and for marriage, the ultimate romantic relationship?

What interests God is not just dating, but who we are when we date, and who we become. What kind of person are you working on becoming, whether you're in a relationship or not? If you're a man, how do you grow in the characteristics needed to be a godly boyfriend, confident in himself, worthy of respect, a selfless protector and generous encourager? If you're a woman, how do you grow in the characteristics needed to be a godly girlfriend, sure of herself and her calling, truly selfless and trustworthy? How do we accept, and even appreciate, being single (for a short time or perhaps long-term) without growing hard-hearted?

This is where our ideas about dating fly in the face of the culture around us. If society says that dating is all about what you can *get*, we say that it is all about what you can *give*. When we just look to our own interests, we lose sight of who we're trying to become. If we're trying to become more like Jesus, then we need to date in a way that demonstrates his radical, revolutionary commitment to putting others before himself.

This needs a romance revolution that starts in the heart:

> Jesus said, 'The first in importance is, "Listen, Israel: The Lord your God is one; so love the Lord God with all your passion and prayer and intelligence and energy." And here is the second: "Love others as well as you love yourself." There is no other commandment that ranks with these.'
> (Mark 12:29–31 *The Message*)

Age-old love

Throughout history, Christians have always stood out in the way they treat other people: whether it was Jesus treating women with respect, or the early church treating slaves with dignity, God has always asked his people to live lives radically different from the society around them. His desire for us to be selfless in our love and committed in our relationships is unchanging. No shift in culture will ever change it.

> Do nothing out of selfish ambition or vain conceit. Rather, in humility value others above yourselves, not looking to your own interests but each of you to the interests of others. In your relationships with one another, have the same mindset as Christ Jesus.
> (Philippians 2:3–5 NIV)

It is because we seek to be Christ-like in our relationships that the church teaches how to be a selfless parent, husband, wife, neighbour, son, daughter, boss, employee, friend. It's time to add 'Christ-like boy/girlfriend' to that list too.

What concerns us with the 'Christian dating' we're seeing is the lack of guidelines. Do you feel this too? Well, we're seeking to change that! At the heart of this book is our desire to see you approach dating from a God-perspective that will change everything: how you feel about dating, how you date and even where your dating leads. It's a bold claim, but did you notice that we didn't promise that you'll get married or be dating within the month? No-one can promise anyone that their special someone is just round the corner. It's an empty promise. It might already ring hollow for you.

So we're not promising that.

What we are promising is to help you be credible, intentional and selfless in your attitude and actions. We believe this is a biblical approach to dating that we can celebrate and practise in the twenty-first century. As we said, this is a book about dating, not marriage. We want to help you value dating in and of itself. It *is* linked to marriage, but we can glorify God and grow as people through our dating experiences.

We're going to explore together what dating God's way could look like for you. Often when we go through hard times in life (at home, work or university), we are quick to see how God can use it to bring us closer to him and to grow us as a person. So why would this not be the same with challenges we face in dating relationships? Why would God not want to help us learn more about ourselves and him through these key relationships in our lives? Should we just say, 'Next time will be different', and never reflect on what went wrong?

Good loving

The dating culture around us wants us to adopt a whole host of values and attitudes, many in opposition to how we are to live as Christ's followers. So in each chapter we will be checking out what God's Word says, and helping you to apply it to your dating in a way that does it justice and allows you to live with integrity:

- Living your life credibly will give you more opportunity to meet someone compatible.
- Approaching your relationship intentionally will give you more opportunities to explore the potential of lifelong partnership with them.
- Choosing to think and act selflessly will give you more opportunities to build this relationship on God's foundations.

So we begin in chapter 1 with a tour of the history of romance and how it has come to dominate our search for happiness and dictate the way we date. Then in chapters 2 and 3, we dig into Scripture and unpack God's heart for all our relationships, especially our romantic ones. Chapters 4 to 7 get into the nitty-gritty of turning God's principles into action, as we consider four important dimensions of dating God's way. Then by chapters 8 and 9, we're ready to talk honestly about sex. Finally, we respond to some of the questions we are asked most often about dating relationships.

We all long for love, for sustained intimacy with someone. But the greatest love any of us will ever know is right here, right now. It's the Father's love, and it reaches us and teaches us how to be all we can be, whether we're single, dating or married. We're encouraging you to be fully engaged in your journey of finding someone to love, but always to remember you are fully God's first.

> Nothing is more practical than finding God, that is, than falling in love in a quite absolute way. What you are in love with, what seizes your imagination, will affect everything. It will decide what will get you out of bed in the morning, what you do with your evenings, how you spend your weekends, what you read, who you know, what breaks your heart, and what amazes you with joy and gratitude. Fall in love, stay in love and it will decide everything. (Pedro Arrupe)[1]

We believe dating can be done well and can please God. It is, however, in need of a radical change: it needs to be infused with a whole new set of values. Our prayer for you as you read our book is that you will be inspired to think wisely, biblically, holistically and selflessly for yourself, your 'dates' and your relationships. But most of all, we pray that you will be open to the life-transforming power of True Love.

> Those who love you are not fooled by mistakes you have made, or dark images you hold about yourself. They remember your beauty when you feel ugly, your wholeness when you are broken, your innocence when you feel guilty, and your purpose when you are confused.
> (Alan Cohen)

Chat room

At the end of each chapter, we've posted some questions in the Chat room for you to consider. We're going to be introducing you to a wide range of teaching from the Bible about relationships, as well as practical ideas and applications. We hope that, when you feel challenged, you'll wrestle with what you're reading and will ask God to reveal what he wants to say to you. Life moves at such a fast pace, so it helps sometimes to stop and reflect on what you're discovering. You might have friends you trust enough to discuss some of these Chat room questions with.

Thinking about dating can throw up a whole load of issues:

- the temptation to make romantic desire the main thing
- the reality of falling in love with a non-Christian
- the dilemma of online dating
- the reality that many of our churches have more single women than single guys
- the wrestle of same-sex attraction

- the pressure on guys to find a girlfriend as a demonstration of manhood
- the pain of being rejected by 'the one'
- the fear of marrying the 'wrong' person
- the worry of being 'left on the shelf'
- the struggles around sexual purity
- the struggle of knowing when you're ready to commit

Take a moment to think about what you're bringing to this book. What are your hopes, questions, heartaches or concerns about dating? What might be behind some of these? You will probably come up with both positive and negative things. That's OK! Being real with yourself is the best place to start in learning how to be real with anyone you date. It's good to take a look at your deeper longings and to bring them to God, asking him to meet you in your deepest place of need.

So why not do that now before you look at the questions below?

- Do you believe you will find 'the one' or make 'the one'? Why?
- How do you tend to act around someone you're attracted to?
- How would you define dating?
- What do you think the purpose of dating is?
- How do you recognize love amidst the multitude of other feelings that go hand in hand with it: infatuation, lust, desperation, attraction, hate?
- How much time do you spend thinking about your future spouse/current boy/girlfriend?
- How often do you ask God to guide you in your relationships?
- Do you find yourself asking him to bring someone along for you to date? How can you begin to change that prayer to asking God to prepare you and teach you about being a good boy/girlfriend?
- What do you hope to get out of reading this book?

CHAPTER ONE:
THE ROMANCE EVOLUTION

I am someone who is looking for love: ridiculous,
inconvenient, consuming, can't live without each other love.
(Carrie in *Sex and the City*)

Logical love

Jim is a regular at my (Rachel's) local coffee shop. He likes to talk
with me at length about his philosophy on love and marriage:
'If someone wants to get married, they will. It's simple. It's about
mind over matter.'

'Wow, Jim. You're quite the romantic,' I reply.

'What's romance got to do with it?' he retorts. 'Have you ever
made a logical, sensible decision based on romantic feelings?
Marriage is too serious to leave to chance.'

He has a point.

Ironically, the café radio, tuned permanently to 'sad-fm',
begins to play 'What's Love Got to Do with It?' 'See,' Jim points
out. 'Tina Turner agrees with me, so I must be right!'

But even with his cheeky grin to soften the blow, it still sounds a bit heartless. Jim's marriage of more than twenty years might be surviving on hard work and sound decisions, but in the words of the mighty Black Eyed Peas, 'Where is the love?' Why on earth would any of us want to marry, let alone date, someone we don't have feelings for?

Where is the love?

So just how important are feelings in making relationships last? And more significantly, how important is that one feeling in particular?

Romance.

It's the feeling we most associate with new relationships. The dictionary defines it as: 'the feeling of excitement and mystery associated with love'. We all know what a romantic gesture looks like (him giving you chocolates or jewellery; her tracking down a signed T-shirt from your favourite sports hero or music band – or vice versa!), but did you know that the high level of importance our culture places on romance hasn't been around that long? It certainly didn't make it into the 'chief-reasons-for-marrying-someone' list until the turn of the last century.

This may surprise you, but it's true. Honest!

We may take for granted our parents' fairly hands-off approach to our romantic adventures (or misadventures!). We may take for granted the deep belief that falling in love with our spouse should come before marriage. We may even take for granted that we can date whoever we want, and even date more than one person if it doesn't work out. But the focus given to those exciting romantic feelings has never been as high or as widespread in any culture or time as it is in our Western culture, right now.

Does that fact matter?

Maybe our relationships look different from those of previous generations, but what's wrong with us wanting to be swept away by love? It's not a crime, or anti-Christian, is it? So what's all the fuss about?

Well, let's put it another way. Our culture loves the idea of falling in love. When we look for a relationship, we fixate on feelings of happiness. But are feelings enough? Can they guarantee the secure, fulfilling and long-lasting relationship that we all want to end up in at some point? Feelings are always subject to change, so if we expect them to act as the foundation, our relationships will probably always be on shaky ground.

> Relationships based on feeling and attraction will not last. People will change physically and personalities will develop. These things will not sustain a relationship.
> (Nigel Pollock)[2]

Whether or not we are aware of it, we are products of the society in which we live. We constantly absorb stories about how we should think and act. Ideas about relationships that were once the norm can change rapidly as society evolves and rethinks its ideas. Changing economies, governments, technologies, beliefs and freedoms can propel a culture to create a totally different way of life. Dating is a great example of this. We have changed from a culture that, in the past, had really strict codes about who should marry who and why, to a culture where any and every consenting relationship (however casual) is actively celebrated. How often have you heard people say something like: 'If it makes them happy, who am I to judge?'

We're not saying that feelings are bad, and we're not saying that when we date we should act like emotionless robots. But how do we make sure that we're being shaped first and foremost by God's view of romance and relationships, rather than by the society around us?

We probably need to start by working out how influenced we actually are by our culture's preoccupation with all things romantic. As Christians, should we focus on feeling 'loved-up' with the person we're dating, or do other things matter more? Should we see romantic feelings we have for someone as indicators that God wants us to date them? Can we ever say that 'falling in love' is part of God's plan for our lives?

Before we get stuck into what the Bible says about relationships, we think it's time for a quick history lesson. Wait! Come back and stop flicking those pages to chapter 2! If we're going to create a romance *revolution*, we need to understand our culture's romance *evolution*. Understanding how our ancestors' search for love has shaped our expectations when we date today is a great place to start. So although this isn't a history book, and we don't have time to look at everything in detail, we hope this helps you understand how the culture around us is affecting your approach to dating. The alternative is being swept along and doing things without getting the chance to think about whether or not we want to go in that direction.

> If you don't create change, change will create you.
> (Gwyneth Paltrow)

The rise of romance

If we look back through human history, it's fair to say that having romantic relationships before you got married was pretty unusual. Although the search for romance occurs at different times throughout history, most cultures have practised arranged marriages, meaning that your parents got to choose who you would spend the rest of your life with. It's really only the modern Western world that has strongly rejected arranged marriage and created a dating culture. Arranged marriages still occur in many societies today, even though parents' involvement varies from culture to culture. In fact, 55% of marriages in the world are thought to be arranged, meaning that less than half of us are free to choose our own marriage partners.[3] But in the West, it goes without saying that marrying for love is the ideal, and the obsession with romance in our pre-married relationships is a modern phenomenon.

Ye olde matrimony

If we wind the clock back by a few thousand years, we can see that throughout the Middle Ages in Europe (around AD 500–1500 or so) marrying your children into wealth and status was often vital for survival (no money meant no life – there were no state benefits). In most cases, the choice of who you married came down to these two things, so looking for romance wasn't a concern for the majority. It's not that being in love *didn't* exist in these cultures. It did, of course. But you didn't expect to fall in love, get romantically swept off your feet, and *then* walk down the aisle. Affectionate feelings (if they came at all) grew *after* marriage, not before.

Marriage was a serious family business, a chance to climb the social ladder and gain financial security. As children, you would have been expected to play your part. Whether your family was stinking rich or dirt poor, everyone knew that a chance to increase wealth and develop family connections mattered:

> If your sister is not yet married, I trust to God that I know how she may be married to a gentleman with an income of 300 marks a year, a great man by birth and good family. If you think you can negotiate anything in this connection please send me word by the bringer of this letter . . .[4]

There would have been some exceptions, of course. We can see that Pope Gratian wrote, 'No woman should be married to anyone except by her free will.'[5] So, in theory, some people may have had a say in the spouse selected for them, but that would have been rare. Money and survival were too important for most people. The idea of marrying the love of your life would have been as alien as us buying a computer that doesn't connect to the internet.

- How would you feel if you were told that romance didn't matter?
- What would you say if you could not make love the main focus in choosing your next date or spouse?
- Why?

Ancient culture just didn't nurture the belief that romance should guide who we end up marrying. So dating didn't happen. After all, why would you need to date if marriage wasn't based on your choice and opinion anyway? People didn't need to get to know their future spouse or search for someone special, so they just didn't need to date. Romance had to take a back seat, but there was about to be a big shake-up!

Let courtship commence

Before we start to play sad songs on the violin for our ancestors, something did start to bubble away in the Middle Ages. A seed was planted that would eventually lead to a change in the importance placed on romance. A new trend called 'courtly love' (*amour courtois*) emerged in the eleventh century in the area around Provence and Burgundy (in modern-day France). Men of noble birth were taught that they needed success in romance in order to be 'real men'. So men, being men, turned this into a competition by showing off their flamboyant fighting and dancing skills for the benefit of the ladies – lucky you. (Not!) These were the original trophy wives, women who knew that, if they wanted to bag the best man, they needed to be rich, gorgeous and out of their suitors' league. One French squire is recorded as having walked to the front of the line of soldiers and, in Spartan-300 style, shouting at the approaching English army:

Is there among you any gentleman who for love of his lady is willing to try me with some feat of arms? If there should be any such, here I am . . . Now look, you English, if there be none among you in love.[6]

You might think this is wildly romantic or complete lunacy, but this wasn't *real* love. It was *idealized* love: fantasy, rather than reality. Wealthy, beautiful women were the object of romantic attention, but this didn't automatically translate into happy relationships. Having men fight over you might sound like heaven, but the ability to hit people and show off isn't a good indicator of a great husband. Having women sit demurely on a pedestal, focusing on their looks and hiding their faults, isn't a good indicator for a great wife either. Since most marriages were still arranged, it was a recipe for disaster.

However, this trend did begin to place the notion of romance into the *pre*-marriage rather than *post*-marriage category. The whiff of romance was in the air, and things slowly began to change in parts of European culture. In Britain, many poets, including Shakespeare, wrote about romantic love during the sixteenth and seventeenth centuries. The world of art and literature helped to spark a new trend that would become firmly established in the eighteenth century and would snowball until the beginning of the twentieth. This trend was known as 'courtship'.

Courtship was revolutionary.

Imagine being stuck in a world where there is no guarantee of being able to talk to someone you fancied, and then all of a sudden you're let loose! Well, maybe not completely. But for the first time ever, Western society began to accept that having feelings for someone *before* you married them mattered, a bit. For example, a beautiful girl could catch a man's eye in public, and he was allowed to pursue her (if there was some money in the bank, and she had a reputation for being a nice girl!). Once he had permission from both families, he could pull out all the stops. You know, take her for walks and write ludicrous love letters.

By the end of the eighteenth century, it was normal to think it was best if you actually liked the person you had to marry (and there's us thinking that was obvious). The importance of romance was on the rise. Some rich families even ended lucrative marriage arrangements because their children failed to create an emotional bond during courtship.[7] Women in Britain could even veto partners selected by their parents.[8] Novels like those of Jane Austen, who published her first book in 1811, exalted marriage for love. Ironically, the very poor, who had little to gain economically in marriage, had more freedom to focus on romantic feelings. If you've got to spend the rest of your life in a hovel with someone, you might as well make sure it's someone you like!

We think courtship began to evolve in the seventeenth century, and this practice lasted right up until the beginning of the twentieth century. It would have looked different at different times, in different classes and cultures, but essentially the Western world began to accept that having romantic feelings for the person you were about to marry was important. The Victorian era (1837–1901), with its boom in wealth from the Industrial Revolution, really solidified this change in Britain. With increased wealth came increased leisure time. And if you were from the richer classes, what better thing to pursue with all this new time and wealth than romance? Courting couples could 'go out' together and buy each other gifts, even if they did have to put up with some ageing aunt to chaperone them. And we thought bumping into your Bible study group leader while on a first date was awkward!

At the heart of courtship was the belief that romance should be explored before marriage, and pre-marriage feelings became more and more important.

You may think that this sounds like dating. Sometimes people think that courtship is just another word for dating, but it isn't. Though courtship was the forerunner of today's dating culture, it was still very restrictive. For starters, courtship wasn't casual, because it signalled publicly the couple's intent to marry one day. They may have been able to get to know each other before marriage, but society saw this as a serious move towards marriage. Cultural standards meant that you certainly didn't 'court' lots of people on your path to finding true love.

Money and status still played a huge part. If their family didn't like you, you weren't going to get a look in. Although interest in romance was rising, society still thought marrying for nothing *but* romance was crazy and would lead to marital unhappiness. Popular literature at the time may have presented marriage as a bed of roses for a couple who were madly in love, but society as a whole never accepted it as the sole justification for marriage. Courting couples had more freedom and *some* space to enjoy premarital romance, but parents, money and families still had a greater say, and the emphasis placed on feelings was still restricted.

- How would you feel if people expected you to marry anyone you tried to chat up?
- How would you feel about being allowed to seek romance with someone, but only if your family approved of them and their bank balance from the start?
- Why would you feel this way?

Courtship allowed romance to rise through the ranks, but it was still a far cry from dating. However, at the beginning of the twentieth century, things changed.

Three, two, one – date!

At the turn of the twentieth century, life as we knew it took a massive turn. Old traditions and customs were replaced with new freedoms. In the 1920s, young men and women were allowed to interact more freely with one another, and with less involvement from their parents. These unsupervised outings, which often happened at the cinema or in dance halls, gave the next generation a lot of freedom, and society was opening up a whole new world when it came to relationships.

This freedom brought a lot of change. Family status and financial needs could be placed 'on hold' while this new form of interaction was happening. Naturally, romance began to take centre stage when it came to forming relationships.

Men and women could also develop pre-marriage relationships with dozens, even hundreds, of different people, whoever they wanted, and they didn't have to commit to them. The relationships could be temporary, and for the first time in history it was accepted in our culture and no-one minded. Everyone was doing it. At the heart of this new cultural practice were two startling beliefs: romance came before marriage, and romantic relationships didn't need to end in marriage.

The restraints of courtship were firmly dropped, and a dating culture emerged.

For the first time ever, society allowed pre-marriage relationships based on feelings, happiness, sexual attraction, compatibility and love. Romance naturally gained more attention and quickly became a driving force.

But even though 'dating' had finally hit the scene, it still had some limitations. Our grandparents didn't date in exactly the same way we do. Romance may have been getting all the attention in choosing who you'd *date*, but *marriage* partners were still influenced by the family's blessing and money. When young women moved from their family home to their married home, their ties to their families were often still very strong. The need for parental inheritance, financial security and childcare on demand saw most newly-weds staying close to their roots. You may have partied your way through a number of dating relationships, but you were still expected to 'settle down' eventually. And when you did, you made sure it was with someone your family liked. After all, they could still disinherit you!

This early dating era gave romance and the couple's feelings an importance that was unrivalled anywhere in history, but other concerns still affected people's choices in the end. However, these concerns became less and less important.

As the century ticked by, women acquired more rights and access to education. Between 1962 and 1980 the number of females who continued in education after the age of eighteen tripled, so, by the 1980s, for the first time, women made up 40% of the student body.[9] This meant more women got jobs, and they relied less and less on their parents' inheritance because they had more of their own money. Cha ching! In fact, during this century a rapid increase in earnings gave both genders more financial opportunity. The average earning for senior professionals, such as doctors, solicitors and dentists, was about £634 a year in 1935 (around £37,000 by today's standards). Yet in the 1980s, civil servants, managers and professionals could earn between £20,000 and £30,000 (around £110,000 by today's standards).[10]

The twentieth century also brought in post-modernity and a focus on the individual. How often do you hear phrases like: 'It's up to them what they do' or 'Do what you think is right for you.' The Western world began to focus on individual desires and experience, whilst rejecting tradition and past wisdom. This meant that, when it came to relationships, parents had to step right back![11]

> You have to try and kill your elders, we have to develop a whole new vocabulary, as indeed is done generation after generation . . . to take the recent past and restructure it in the way that we felt we had authorship of.
> (David Bowie on the Ziggy era, early 1970s)[12]

Essentially, early freedom allowed dating and romance to receive loads of attention, and by the end of the century dating and romance had gained even more importance. People could date whoever they wanted, and because they were educated, financially independent and encouraged to think individualistically, this allowed them to turn a dating partner into a spouse, even if their parents didn't agree. Dating and romance were now on top.

- What do you think about our growing dependence on romantic feelings?
- If you could turn back the clock, would you?
- Why or why not?

Romancipation?

It's fascinating to see the rise of romance and how it goes hand in hand with dating. We now have a dating culture because Western societies accept that:

1. We are free to choose whoever we want as boy/girlfriend or spouse.
2. Relationships are allowed (often expected) to be temporary and non-committal.
3. Romantic desire or 'falling in love' is the most important ingredient in any (new) relationship.

'Dating' might go by lots of different names: 'going out', 'hooking up', 'getting together', 'going steady', 'seeing someone'. But whatever we call it, dating is always about two people looking for and fostering an emotional bond. By its very definition, it doesn't need to be exclusive or committed, and if it's not satisfying, end it!

Today nothing receives more attention in popular media than romance. We love the idea of falling in love. Nearly every song is about being in love – or losing it. Every good film needs romance, whether it's a chick flick obsessed with 'the one', or an action movie where the hero gets the villain and the girl thrown in for good measure, or the kids' story with the happily-ever-after ending. Magazines and newspapers are filled with tips for finding love, and a whole industry rotates around celebrities' love lives. Closer to home, social media provides us with immediate updates on friends' relationship statuses, complete with snaps of their happy moments. Everything is telling us that romance rules and that, without this kind of love, we can't be happy. The rise of romance has made love and romantic relationships the meaning of life.

But our focus on romance has its problems. In her sequel to *Eat, Pray, Love*, author Elizabeth Gilbert travels the world, exploring attitudes to love and marriage. Her discovery is that:

> Whenever a conservative culture of arranged marriage is replaced by an expressive culture of people choosing their own partners based on love, divorce rates will immediately begin to sky rocket . . . about five minutes after people start clamouring for the right to choose their own spouses based on love, they will begin clamouring for the right to divorce those spouses once that love has died.[13]

Romance is something that looks good in the shop, but when you take it home it can sometimes be a bit of a let-down.

The side effects can't be ignored. Dating in a way that focuses *primarily* on romantic feelings makes the relationship more likely to be fragile, haphazard and selfish.

Relationships become fragile because feelings are always shifting and changing. If people believe that relationships are only 'successful' when they have romantic feelings, then when those feelings are lost, or weaken, what happens to the relationship? The result is a rise in the divorce rate in recent times, which has clearly risen overall in the last fifty years.

They become haphazard because valuing feelings above commitment can leave the relationship in a kind of no man's land. Instead of intentionally and selflessly investing in their relationship, people think, 'I'll see how I feel.' Thinking this, or 'It's not serious or anything; we just like each other', means that no-one knows where they stand.

They become more selfish because, in the end, you're focused on how you feel and what you want, and the relationship just rolls along unintentionally with no defined purpose or commitment. It also breeds a selfish attitude towards relationships and to each other: 'I'll date as long as I am happy'; 'I'll only commit to you as long as I want to. If it gets hard, it's over.'

The sociologist Zygmunt Bauman asserts, 'Love is a mortgage loan drawn on an uncertain, and inscrutable, future.'[14]

Dating lots of people, and pursuing temporary relationships in search of an 'emotional high', can cause damage. We can end up feeling hurt, rejected and lonely. So if dating this way is causing so much heartache and insecurity in relationships, should a romance revolution do away with romance altogether, or is there another way?

Dating God's way

Before you slope off to a monastery and vow never to think about romance or dating again, take a deep breath. We believe that romance *is* a gift from God. Love between a man and a woman can be a wonderful blessing to them and to those around them. Romance matters, so it's good to enjoy it. But we reckon we need to rethink the role our culture says it should play in our relationships. It's possible to harness the best that romance has to offer and date really well. But this kind of dating requires a God-perspective: a commitment to radical relationship building! At times it will fly in the face of popular opinion or advice. It might even require personal sacrifice and facing up to difficult decisions. But what we can say for sure is that it will honour God.

In seeking to live honourable lives, some Christians have sought to avoid dating altogether, but we believe it's not dating that is the problem, but rather the *way* we date. Imagine if we saw dating as part of our witness to Jesus? There's nothing stopping us from demonstrating genuine care for others, as well as a deep commitment to God, while we're dating. If we made sacrificial Christ-like love the starting point for romance and dating, as risky as that sounds, it would start a revolution. People would have to sit up and take notice!

Good dating begins with getting our hearts right with God. The psalmist asks,

> How can a young person live a clean life?
>> By carefully reading the map of your Word.
> I'm single-minded in pursuit of you;
>> don't let me miss the road signs you've posted.
> I've banked your promises in the vault of my heart
>> so I won't sin myself bankrupt.
> Be blessed, GOD;
>> train me in your ways of wise living.
> (Psalm 119:9–16 *The Message*)

Sometimes the questions about romantic relationships that we level at the Bible (Can I date a non-Christian? Why can't we have sex when we love each other?) are less about us wanting to know *God's* plan for our lives and more about us wanting him to approve *our* plan for our lives. Does this demonstrate sacrificial love? When we committed to following Jesus, we joined the team whose mission is to seek God first and join him in restoring his world. This will inspire, challenge and fulfil us in ways we can only begin to imagine. It's an active, not a passive, lifestyle. We're no longer on the sidelines waiting for our lives to begin. We're signed up to learning the hard lessons of selflessness in all our relationships. We're committed to being a faithful friend, generous neighbour, forgiving sibling, humble employee and an honourable girl/boyfriend. None of this happens without obedience to Jesus and an acceptance that we will make mistakes along the way. Thank God for grace!

> You learned Christ! My assumption is that you have paid careful attention to him, been well instructed in the truth precisely as we

have it in Jesus. Since, then, we do not have the excuse of ignorance, everything – and I do mean everything – connected with that old way of life has to go. It's rotten through and through. Get rid of it! And then take on an entirely new way of life – a God-fashioned life, a life renewed from the inside and working itself into your conduct as God accurately reproduces his character in you.
(Ephesians 4:20–24 *The Message*)

Single, dating or married – these are all times when we can explore God's will for us and his deep desire to build godly character into us. Trusting that God knows the desires of our hearts, and will give us good gifts that satisfy, means that we can have every confidence when we date. The outcome is not just down to us. Our lasting happiness is not dependent on us finding romance. We have a God who will work in and through our dating relationships. He will give us the courage to see ourselves honestly and to take the responsibility of changing to become a better boy/girlfriend.

The dating culture we know is recent and has evolved over time. Romance had never been so central. Whether we like it or not, this culture has affected, and continues to affect, us and our choices. Do we like what we see? Do we realize that, as well as the good that being free to choose who to date offers us, there are also things that with God's help we could change for our benefit and his glory?

Our romance revolution begins with a celebration of God's incredible love for us. He is the God who desires, pursues and wins us! His freely given love brings out the best in us. When we allow this to overflow into our search for lasting love with someone, we find ourselves acting more like him, and less like the culture around us.

When I went to uni, I dated on my terms and slept around and got hurt a lot and damaged other people. Recently I have come

back to God and surrendered my life to him. It's so much better now, and I have hope for my future relationships.
(David)

Chat room

- Have you recently celebrated God's love for you, which comes with no hidden motives?
- How could you make this a part of your daily life?
- How important is romance to you?
- What attracts you to the people you like?
- How do you involve God in thinking about your relationships? If you don't involve him at all, how could you start to do so?
- Do you find arranged marriage or courtship more appealing than dating? Why?
- What is your response to our suggestion that you can be part of a new dating agenda that could impact on society and ultimately save people, yourself included, from a lot of hurt?
- A romanticized approach can make us put people on pedestals, which they are bound to fall off! Have you ever been guilty of 'worshipping' someone you're attracted to?
- Can you think of relationships that have been built on the fragile foundations of an unintentional and selfish attitude to dating?
- When you think about going out with someone, how much of a priority do you give to having your needs met?
- If you're in a relationship, on what do you base the strength of your relationship? What role do feelings play in that?
- What do you think is helpful or distracting about our culture's focus on romance?

CHAPTER TWO:
FRAME IT

There are two primary choices in our lives: to accept conditions as they exist or to accept the responsibility for changing them.
(Denis Waitley, motivational speaker)[15]

The tale of two approaches

'At the roundabout, take the second exit.' 'In 100 yards, turn right.' 'You have reached your destination.' When sat navs first came out, I (André) thought they were amazing: a little black box with the answers to all my deep and challenging questions – well, the geography-related ones anyway! There is something reassuring about travelling with a voice that tells you exactly what to do and when to do it. It's great knowing nothing can go wrong. Unless you go round a corner and it detaches from the brace and rolls under the car seat: I can assure you that's not fun. But if we put those sticky situations aside, nifty gadgets that tell us every little move to make can give us the promise of security, even if in reality we know that life isn't always quite so clear-cut.

Most of us like a bit more room to manoeuvre! We like to be a bit creative and do our own thing in our own way. Do you have an annoyingly super-talented friend who can sit down with a blank canvas and some bog-standard paints and turn it into a jaw-dropping masterpiece? To us a blank canvas is a blank canvas, but to them it provides a multitude of possibilities. They can turn it into *anything* they want.

Well, sometimes the way we read the Bible and do theology can be summarized as blank canvas versus sat nav.

And yes, when we talk about people doing theology, we are talking about you! It's not a word reserved for people who lock themselves away to study old books. Every disciple of Jesus is a theologian. If you ever ask the big questions about your faith, if you wrestle with how to live God's way in the twenty-first century, if you read the Bible to get to know God more, then you're a theologian. The Bible anchors our understanding of who we are as God's people and helps us to see things as God sees them. The challenge for us when we read the Bible, then, is not just to ask whether we believe it, but whether we believe *through* it; whether we allow it to influence how we live.

Let's be honest, there's always a chance that we may fall into the trap of applying what the Bible says incorrectly. Sometimes we treat it like a blank canvas and act as if the Bible has nothing relevant to say to us today, so we're free to do as we please. We act as if we can turn it into anything we want to and live any way we please. We met someone recently who had this view of the Bible. After a seminar we ran about choosing God's boundaries for our relationships, she told us that to her being a Christian meant having a 'personal Jesus' whose one desire was to make her happy. She felt that having sex with guys made her happy, so she couldn't understand why Jesus would ask her to wait for marriage. She couldn't believe that God's way contradicted her way of living. In trying to hold on so tightly to life the way she wanted it, she was unable to see that, when we 'lose' it to Jesus, we actually gain it in abundance! 'If you grasp and cling to life on your terms, you'll lose it, but if you let that life go, you'll get life on God's terms' (Luke 17:33 *The Message*).

But there's another way we can wrongly apply the Bible, and that's when we treat it like a sat nav. Although, for example, Exodus 35 – 40 goes into minute detail about how to set up a tent, there are no specific directions about what to do in *every* situation that could *ever* occur. The challenge for us is to uncover the Bible's unchanging truths, and to discern how to apply them in our culture that is hooked on social networking and reality TV. By reading the whole of God's Word, we discover his patterns for living are as applicable today as they were back then: 'For the word of God is alive and active. Sharper than any double-edged sword, it penetrates even to dividing soul and spirit, joints and marrow' (Hebrews 4:12 NIV).

So how should we read the Bible? We're not talking about where you sit or what translation to use, but how you can apply the eternal and relevant truth of the Bible to your life.

Unfinished masterpiece

We think that a great way to approach the Bible is by imagining it as an unfinished painting. It's not unfinished, and our task is never to improve or rewrite Scripture. But imagine you're standing in front of an easel with a half-done oil painting on it. You can see that, although some great artist has already painted a beautiful border to frame the picture and done a few sketches across the middle to mark where he is going, the middle still needs work. To the right is a table covered with paint pots and brushes, and a post-it note that reads, 'Please keep painting. The Artist'. You are being invited to pick up the paintbrushes and *continue* his masterpiece.

The artist invites us to faithfully interpret what's gone before. If his border was made up of blues, greens and greys, then we're not being faithful to his vision if we start using bright pink in the middle. Likewise, we think God has invited us to take his Word and its eternal unchanging truth, and apply it faithfully and relevantly to the new culture that surrounds us, in order to glorify him.

> The Bible is not primarily a proof text or a doctrinal statement; it is a drama. It is not only theology; it is a poem. It is not only facts; it is an adventure. The biblical story is a captivating read that should leave us breathless.
> (Spring Harvest 2010: Route 66 Theme Guide)

God, as the great Author of Scripture, invites us to see what has gone before, and apply it faithfully and authentically to our current culture. He wants us to use the borders to guide us as we paint the middle of the canvas. History is full of Christians who have sought to do this in their time and culture, and so have thrown themselves into playing their part in God's great ongoing drama. Significant social movements were led by people who were first grabbed by God's Word and Spirit, and then seized a moment in history to change things. We're talking about revolutionaries like William Wilberforce, Jackie Pullinger, Martin Luther King, Gladys Aylward. Through their intimate knowledge of the Scriptures, they learnt to love what God loves, and to stand against those things God stands against, be it poor housing, racism or human trafficking.

> If to be feelingly alive to the sufferings of my fellow-creatures is to be a fanatic, I am one of the most incurable fanatics ever permitted to be at large.
> (William Wilberforce)

Imagine using this approach when studying what the Bible might say about dating. This becomes significant, because the Bible says nothing about dating! So if we're turning to the Bible to find a dating manual, we would have to say that the Bible has nothing relevant to teach us. However, if we seek to interpret faithfully what the Bible teaches about relationships, then we will discover a whole wealth of wisdom for dating.

God is inviting you to throw yourself into this process, to see dating as he sees it. A biblical framework will enable this, and will give you security and success in your relationships. This doesn't mean that you won't be heartbroken by someone, or that you'll meet the right person within seconds of putting this book down. But if the Bible reveals God's unchanging design for human relationships, then choosing a biblical approach to dating will give you the best possible chance of finding lasting love.

We hope you'll discover how choosing to date within a Bible-based framework will help you to:

- truly be yourself, whether dating or single
- grow in your knowledge and love of God
- get a clear idea of whether your dating relationship can go the distance
- practise the skills needed for the life-long partnership of marriage
- see dating as a holy and godly experience, rather than something you just drift in and out of
- understand how God's plan for your life isn't dependent on your finding someone to love
- put God's mission first, and experience the deepest satisfaction you could ever hope for

So how can we make a biblical case for something that never existed in Bible times? If the Bible says nothing directly about dating, how can we come up with relevant theories to help you uphold biblical principles when you're falling madly in love with someone?

Begin with the borders

Just as an artist uses a distinctive palette of colours to create the borders of the painting, the Bible presents some core ideas that are fundamental to framing our understanding of all our relationships. Getting hold of this will allow us to pursue dating in a way that does justice to God's unchanging ideals for relationships.

Another good question to ask is: 'How would Jesus date?' OK, he didn't date, fall in love or get married. But when we say that Jesus set us an example that we should follow, none of us thinks we should be walking around with beards and leather sandals: that's optional! It must mean something else, and that something else is all about character.

- How would Jesus want me to treat my boyfriend?
- How might Jesus want me to end my relationship?
- What might Jesus say about my need for a girlfriend?

The danger for many of us today is that we coast along with such a shallow knowledge of the Bible (although we're keen to learn more), that we struggle even to begin to think about glorifying God through our romantic relationships. This is why it's essential we study Scripture for practical guidance (how should I act?), as well as theological insight (what does this tell me about God's character and heart?).

We hope you are ready to begin painting with us. Feel free to put on a French beret if it helps! We are about to delve into some of the Bible's rich teaching on intimate relationships, and on relationships in general. What can we learn and how can that shape our dating?

Be active

God is more involved in your life than you will ever realize. He is more invested in your flourishing than you will ever be. And as he knows what's best for you, he wants you to grow up into the man or woman he gave you the potential to be. But he doesn't do the growing up for you. Imagine being a parent who wants their kid to do well in school. What a good parent you are! But let's imagine that your way of helping your kid do well is to do all their homework for them. How would that help them grow in skills and knowledge? How would that help them really work out what they are capable of? It would be better to support them in doing their homework when they are little, so that, as they grow older, they can manage for themselves, but with the benefit of your encouragement.

We believe that God, the ultimate Good Parent, takes this approach with us. As the Creator and Sustainer of all things, he wants us to be active, not passive, in living this one, wild life he has given us. There may not be any instances of dating as we know it in Bible times, but there are many stories of intimate relationships where the people involved made decisions to make something happen. This is why our first 'be' is 'be active'. Take a look at how these famous couples decided to 'be active' in their relationships:

Adam 4 Eve
In Genesis 1 – 2, we read not only about God creating the physical world, but also how he created us to live within it. It's a blueprint for relational dynamics between God and his created world, not just a record of the physical creation. In Genesis 2:18, we read, 'The LORD God said, "It is not good for the man to be alone. I will make a helper suitable for him" ' (NIV), showing God's design for human relationships. We are meant to have friends and seek companionships. Romantic relationships are no exception. There is nothing wrong with wanting to find someone to spend the rest of your life with. God created us with an inbuilt longing for sustained intimacy with someone. Yet the story continues:

Now the LORD God had formed out of the ground all the wild animals and all the birds in the sky. He brought them to the man to see what he would name them; and whatever the man called each living creature, that was its name. So the man gave names to all the livestock, the birds in the sky and all the wild animals. But for Adam no suitable helper was found. So the LORD God caused the man to fall into a deep sleep; and while he was sleeping, he took one of the man's ribs and then closed up the place with flesh. Then the LORD God made a woman from the rib he had taken out of the man, and he brought her to the man. The man said,

> 'This is now bone of my bones
>   and flesh of my flesh;
> she shall be called "woman",
>   for she was taken out of man.'
> (Genesis 2:19–23 NIV)

If we look closely, what we see is Adam *involved* in finding a wife. Can you picture the scene? As God brings the animals to Adam to be named, Adam wonders if any of them will be the kind of companion he is aching for: his equal, a creature like him but different. But unsurprisingly, Adam said 'no' to all of them. (We think the blind date with the alligator would have been a bit awkward!)

What is God doing here? If he knows that Adam needs Eve, why doesn't he just go ahead and make her? 'Hey, Adam, I know what you need. So here's Eve. She's nice – you'll like her!' Well, God, who is able to do anything, chooses to involve Adam in the process instead. Adam wasn't meant just to sit back as God did the hard work. He let Adam be part of the search. God didn't make Eve, bring her to him and say, 'This is your wife.' Rather, Adam said, 'This is bone of my bone . . . ' Adam's response to seeing Eve for the first time is heartfelt and freely given. 'Look, she's like me, but different. She's mine and I'm hers, for life.' It's powerful, erotic stuff! Undeniably, God was heavily involved as

Creator, but Adam was an active player in the process. He wasn't just sitting around with his feet up, watching the footy. He was out searching, discovering what a suitable helper would be like, learning when to say no and when to say yes. And when he found her, boy was he happy!

Isaac 4 Rebekah

We see God inviting people to be involved in their relationships again in Genesis. It's a story that people sometimes use to prove that God will magic up the perfect person for us. But nothing could be further from the truth.

> He [Isaac] went out to the field one evening to meditate, and as he looked up, he saw camels approaching. Rebekah also looked up and saw Isaac. She got down from her camel and asked the servant, 'Who is that man in the field coming to meet us?'
>
> 'He is my master,' the servant answered. So she took her veil and covered herself.
>
> Then the servant told Isaac all he had done. Isaac brought her into the tent of his mother Sarah, and he married Rebekah. So she became his wife, and he loved her; and Isaac was comforted after his mother's death.
>
> (Genesis 24:63–67 NIV)

If we only read these five verses, we would think God was being a matchmaker: Isaac spots Rebekah, and boom, they get married. However, in this chapter (which is actually sixty-seven verses long) people are constantly taking the initiative and making decisions.

Abraham considers what Isaac needs in a wife and gives strict instructions to his servant (24:3–4), who then goes off and jumps through a lot of hoops to make sure he gets the right woman. Rebekah could have said no to leaving so soon, but instead she said yes when given the choice (24:56–59). You could argue that, because it was an arranged marriage, the couple didn't have much say in the matter. Maybe they didn't have a choice in the way we understand it today, but they were obviously willing participants, because we read about the feeling of love and comfort between them (24:67). Isaac entered into the marriage willingly and happily. Throughout the story, God is heavily involved, but the individuals are still actively seeking to honour God in their choices. We can't use the last bit of the story as permission to sit and wait for Mr or Mrs Charming to arrive, however tempting that may be.

Jacob 4 Rachel

We read of another famous relationship later in Genesis (chapter 29 and the following chapters). Jacob and Rachel get hitched eventually, but right from the start it's obvious that 'struggle' would define this relationship. After their first kiss, Jacob cries hysterically, tells her they're related, and she runs off! But the attraction of this relationship lies in just how long Jacob has to wait for Rachel. We read about a love-sick man, working tirelessly for seven years to impress Laban, his father-in-law-to-be, before he could marry Laban's daughter Rachel. Talk about a labour of love! I (André) struggle with seven minutes of shopping! After seven years of hard graft, Jacob is tricked into marrying the wrong daughter (Leah) and has to work *another* seven years for Rachel's hand in marriage. Jacob, Laban, Rachel, Leah, Jacob's later wives and many children argue their way throughout the rest of Genesis. Jealousy, resentment and bitterness rage in this family. There is no happily-ever-after ending. Like many of the episodes of family life in the Bible, this story challenges any idea that God will sort everything out for us while we sit back and take it easy, that we will find 'the one' and our troubles will be over. Biblically, that just isn't the case. God expects us to be active players for the welfare of our families and relationships. This dysfunctional family shows us that we have to be active. 'Happily-ever-afters' are not automatic; we must learn to sort out problems in our relationships.

Ruth 4 Boaz

Here's another powerful story of individuals making plans and godly choices for their relationships, within the limits of their culture. Naomi, her husband and their two sons were from Bethlehem, but when famine came they were forced to go to Moab. Naomi's sons married Moabite women called Ruth and Orpah. But tragedy struck; her sons and husband died, leaving her widowed and childless. Orpah returned to her family, but Ruth vowed to stay with Naomi, even though that meant leaving her own country and settling in Bethlehem, in a foreign land. It might seem like a strange decision for a young woman to make. But the fact that this story of two poor women gets into the Bible at all is a sign of just how impressive and godly their selfless attitude and proactive lifestyle are. To make ends meet, Ruth takes to collecting food by picking up the scraps that the workers leave behind in their fields. It's risky work for a young, single and poor woman, who might have been attacked by field workers. But she has the good fortune of finding a barley field owned by Boaz, a long-lost relative of Naomi's. He instructs his men to keep their hands off her.

> Then Ruth bowed low with her face to the ground and said to him, 'I am not an Israelite. Why have you been so kind to notice me?'
>
> Boaz answered her, 'I know about all the help you have given your mother-in-law after your husband died. You left your father and mother and your own country to come to a nation where you did not know anyone. May the Lord reward you for all you have done. May your wages be paid in full by the Lord, the God of Israel, under whose wings you have come for shelter.'
> (Ruth 2:10–12 NCV)

Eventually they end up marrying. We know it is not the best ever chat-up line, but it seems to have done the trick! When I (Rachel) heard this story in Sunday school, I thought it sounded like a fairy tale: Ruth, the beautiful but poor woman, trapped in her mean mother-in-law's house, is finally rescued by the handsome prince, Boaz. But this isn't what happened at all. Ruth isn't a passive princess in a tower; she's a bold woman who sees in Boaz a good man who can offer the kind of protection she and Naomi need. She introduces the idea of marriage to Boaz, and being a man of integrity, Boaz agrees to marry her, after speaking to the necessary people and following the right procedures (Ruth 3 – 4).

We don't know if Ruth was pretty or Boaz was handsome; we do know that both of them were ready to act when they needed to. They go down in biblical history not only as blood ancestors of Jesus, but as character ancestors, with the same kind of compassion and integrity that Jesus showed. Their relationship was not just about feelings and their own interests; rather, it was based on the rhythms of God's desires. They were active, honourable, God-seeking participants in the story of God – not passengers.

God's way = the best way

We can see God at work in all these relationships. But we also see the importance of people being prepared to take responsibility (which doesn't always happen in Bible stories) in their intimate relationships within their cultural context. It should encourage us to see that, like us, our ancestors in the faith sometimes got things right, and sometimes they got things wrong. But God still worked out his plan through them.

This gives us the first clear idea, the first section of the border that frames the 'painting'. Being active in our relationships *doesn't* mean ignoring God's way and doing things our own way. Quite the opposite. Being active in our relationships means asking ourselves questions about the kind of person we are (dating or single) and the kind of relationships we create. It means learning how to become someone who reflects God's glory, whether we're in a relationship or not. Do we glorify God through our relationships or lose sight of God when a new romance is on the scene?

This may be a good time to ask yourself:

- When it comes to finding someone to go out with, have I been waiting for God to bring the right person to me? Why?
- In what ways could I become more active in developing my character?
- In what ways could I become more active in taking responsibility for the relationship I am in/want to be in?

Be selfless

Our second 'be' sums up everything the Bible teaches about how we should act in any and all of our relationships: be selfless.

When we analyse the Bible's wider teaching on relationships, we discover that it constantly encourages us to be selfless, to put others first in all our relationships. All the commands are about being other-centred instead of self-centred. Thinking about other people's needs before our own. Loving those around us. When Jesus was asked what was the most important command, he declared, 'Hear, O Israel: the Lord our God, the Lord is one. Love the Lord your God with all your heart and with all your soul and with all your mind and with all your strength. . . . Love your neighbour as yourself' (Mark 12:29–31 NIV).

Jesus makes it clear that creating loving relationships with others can't be separated from our love for God. Selfishness and love can't go hand in hand. Hidden motives and genuine friendship can't co-exist. We demonstrate our love for God by putting others before ourselves. Love God. Love your neighbour, be selfless and put them before yourself. This is the greatest command and it sums up the whole law. Love God and love your neighbour from your very core. It should be in our very DNA!

In his last piece of recorded teaching to his disciples before his death, Jesus again gives the command that people must love one another (John 15:12). Jesus wants us to love everyone, even our enemies (Matthew 5:43–48). More importantly, his actions backed up his words. He formed relationships with any who were willing. Jesus loved people because he loved them, not because he wanted to use them or get something in return. Unlike the Pharisees and religious people of his day, Jesus would deliberately seek fellowship with sinners and outsiders (Mark 2:15–17), putting the needs of others before his own.

Most of all, the cross is the ultimate demonstration of radical, self-giving, selfless love to God and neighbour.

The New Testament authors return to this theme again and again. Paul writes,

> For you have been called to live in freedom, my brothers and sisters. But don't use your freedom to satisfy your sinful nature. Instead, use your freedom to serve one another in love. For the whole law can be summed up in this one command: 'Love your neighbour as yourself.' But if you are always biting and devouring one another, watch out! Beware of destroying one another. (Galatians 5:13–15 NLT)

We don't want to fall into the trap of self-indulgence, which destroys us and those around us. Being a follower of Christ means following his example and showing love to others, even when it is costly. Paul says Jesus breaks the dividing wall of fear and mistrust between Gentiles and Jews (Ephesians 2:14–18). Jesus' sacrifice means there is no longer any ranking system within churches or between people, and with this comes the freedom to serve and love one another: 'And he has given us this command: Those who love God must also love their Christian brothers and sisters' (1 John 4:21 NLT).

Can you hear the command loud and clear?

'Be selfless! Be selfless! Be selfless!'

Treat other people as you want to be treated; consider their interests. Don't move only in the circles that benefit your popularity or career. Don't invest in someone just to see what you can get out of it.

Do nothing out of selfish ambition or vain conceit. Rather, in humility value others above yourselves, not looking to your own interests but each of you to the interests of the others. In your relationships with one another, have the same mindset as Christ Jesus.
(Philippians 2:3–5 NIV)

Love like Jesus.

Be selfless like Jesus.

Treat the people you go out with like Jesus would treat them.

He sets the bar high, doesn't he? Our Christ-likeness can and should be shown in how we date someone. In fact, if it isn't, then we're not ready to start dating. This is why Paul encourages us to have the same attitude as Christ in all things.

Think of yourselves the way Christ Jesus thought of himself. He had equal status with God but didn't think so much of himself that he had to cling to the advantages of that status no matter what. Not at all . . . Instead, he lived a selfless, obedient life . . .
(Philippians 2:5–8 *The Message*)

Nothing new in this Testament

But this idea isn't new. The Old Testament authors understood that God's laws were meant to single out his people as a community known for their selflessness, concern for the poor and commitment to pursuing justice. The foreigner is to be treated like a companion (Leviticus 19:18, 33–34), ill-treatment of the weak and disabled is forbidden (19:14) and dishonest gain is always wrong (19:35–36). The Ten Commandments might sound like a load of 'don'ts', but in fact they are all about maintaining healthy relationships with God (the first four) and with others (the final six). The prophets were often hated because they spoke out against selfishness and greed:

He has shown you, O mortal, what is good.
    And what does the LORD require of you?
To act justly and to love mercy
    and to walk humbly with your God.
(Micah 6:8 NIV)

Sadly, even with all these instructions, the people of Israel were often self-seeking. Sometimes the Bible tells us what a good relationship should look like by showing us a bad one. Stories of people making selfish decisions litter the pages of Scripture. Unlike the Law or the Prophets, which define sins clearly and speak against them, stories of real families and their failures don't always point to the kind of relationships God wants us to have. Some are good models to be imitated, but most show us the mess that happens when people reject God's way of relating to one another.

Look at these examples of selfishness: Abram's cowardice puts his wife in danger (Genesis 12:10–20); Rebekah and Jacob's deception changes their family's lives forever (27:5–45); Shechem rapes Dinah (34:1–2); and Judah ends up sleeping with his daughter-in-law Tamar (chapter 38). These examples demonstrate how we shouldn't treat one another!

So the second idea that frames our 'painting' is to 'be selfless'. It's not simply a nice idea; it's a life-changing one!

No relationship is exempt from this. The Bible always calls for selflessness in *all* relationships. So it would naturally follow that modern relationships, like dating, must also be guided by this principle if we are to do God's Word justice today.

Your priority as a Christian boy/girlfriend is to love your partner as God loves them. Whoever chooses to date you should have the same priority.

Above all the grace and the gifts that Christ gives to his beloved is that of overcoming self.
(St Francis of Assisi)

When Becca, who is now my (André's) fiancée, and her friends were deciding what uni to go to, a lot of their boyfriends wanted them to stay in London. They didn't fancy a long-distance relationship. Becca thought I might have reacted in the same way. Instead, I asked her to pick the uni she felt God had called her to. I assured her that, wherever it was, we would make it work. For me, seeking to be a selfless boyfriend has meant putting her needs and God's will before mine. I'd have loved to have her close by, but that's not what she felt called to. I could have sulked about it or trusted God. It was hard, but we chose trust.

It's inspiring to hear stories of couples becoming more selfless in their relationships. One of our friends cleaned his girlfriend's dirty bathroom. A little bit extreme? We think it's great. He didn't do it because he enjoyed it, or because he wanted to, but because she was really busy and stressed. He wanted to support her and express his deep love for her. Selflessness like this, in big things and little things, always glorifies God.

The big picture

So our guiding principle as we date is always to be active and selfless. This is God's desire and his design. As we 'paint', we need to do so in a way that does justice to God's big picture. Imagine having a boy/girlfriend who puts God first, demonstrates selflessness in how they treat you and is active in their choices about the relationship. Imagine being like that yourself. Then imagine this attitude spilling out into all of your relationships.

Chat room

Being passive

Can you identify any ways you have become passive in your relationships – in attitude or actions? We've suggested some to get you started. How could you turn a passive attitude into an active attitude or action?

Passive attitude	Active attitude
God will show me who I will marry.	What type of person should I look for? What makes a godly man/woman?
He/she will come along and it will be easy.	How can I improve my character now?
I will not do anything I don't like doing.	How can I serve my friend/boyfriend/girlfriend today?
I will not take responsibility for why we argue all the time.	What do I do that causes problems or tensions? How can I replace this with healthy habits?

Being selfish

The harder job might be to challenge our own selfishness. Let's face it, selfishness can often go undetected or unchallenged. In today's culture, a selfish attitude is often applauded. 'They know what they want and aren't afraid to go for it!' could describe someone who always wants their own way and quickly moves on from friends or dates who dare to challenge them.

- If you were to ask people who know you well how you're doing in the whole area of being selfless, how might they respond?
- Are you able to ask God to highlight areas of your life where your attitude or behaviour is selfish rather than selfless? This might involve accepting his forgiveness and moving forward.
- Who could you be accountable to, as you learn to practise a selfless life?
- Being selfless and being a doormat are not the same thing. How can you make sure that you are aware of the difference in your relationship?

- Have you been on the receiving end of someone's selfishness recently? How did it feel? How do you handle your own selfishness? Have you been selfish towards someone else recently? How could you make sure it doesn't happen again?

We justify our actions by appearances;
    God examines our motives.
Clean living before God and justice with our neighbours
    mean far more to God than religious performance.
(Proverbs 21:2–3 *The Message*)

CHAPTER THREE:
HIGH HOPES

Every relationship I've been in, I've overwhelmed the girl.
They just can't handle all the love.
(Justin Timberlake)

Overwhelming

Poor Justin Timberlake. Imagine lavishing all your love on women, only to realize that they will never fully appreciate all you've got to give! We men can have it so tough sometimes. (Yeah, right!)

Whether his approach to relationships is helpful or not, Justin reminds us of something very important: love is overwhelming. People do incredible, crazy, even stupid things when they love, especially when that love carries with it the promise of romance. A seventy-year-old man was recently discovered in a cave in China that he and his wife had escaped to fifty years earlier. Over that time, he had hand-carved six thousand stairs up the mountainside to their secret home, just for her convenience!

No wonder we have high hopes for our romantic adventures. Sometimes it's hard to keep these longings in check when we meet someone we're attracted to. Whether it's a text from someone we've just met or a declaration of undying love after a month of dating, we expect love to deliver certain things and to *feel* a certain way.

It can lift us up, sweep us away, make us smile, turn us inside out and our lives upside down. It can make us nervous, put us off our food, keep us awake at night, distract us from work and take our breath away! Loving someone can feel like a miracle and a nightmare at the same time. It doesn't seem to follow any rules. Why did I fall for them, when on paper that other person looked so much better for me? How is it that we were friends for years, and then suddenly, out of nowhere, I found myself really attracted to them? Why do I always fall for the people who don't fall for me?

But not only can falling in love with someone feel uncertain, it can also feel risky. Wanting to be loved for who we are, but not knowing what might happen if we let someone in, requires courage. Being real with our feelings might take us on a roller-coaster ride of hopes raised and dashed, but how many of us want to jump off that ride and never risk getting close to someone again? Here's one of the most beautiful verses in the Bible about the power of love:

> Place me like a seal over your heart,
>   like a seal on your arm;
> for love is as strong as death,
>   its jealousy unyielding as the grave.
> It burns like blazing fire,
>   like a mighty flame.
> Many waters cannot quench love;
>   rivers cannot sweep it away.
> (Song of Solomon 8:6–7 NIV)

It's amazing to think that God has created us with a capacity to love like this, to burn with a passion for someone. Calling love overwhelming may be a bit of an understatement! If this picture of love is in the Bible, what does it say about the love God has created us with the capacity to experience, not just with him, but with another person? It's because the feelings associated with loving someone *can* be so intense and create *such* deep connections, that it shouldn't surprise us that God wants it to be contained within a strong relationship. As far as he is concerned, the relationship created to nurture and keep love like this is marriage.

'We knew it!' we can hear some of you shouting. 'You're going to tell us to date only someone we know we're going to marry!'

Don't worry, we're not! For us, dating isn't a new kind of courtship or arranged marriage.

But as we're already discovering, dating God's way will see us living by a different set of standards from those of the world around us. These standards are shaped by the type of relationships celebrated in Scripture. So before your heart palpitations get too much, don't panic; we are not about to make you slap a ring on your finger. Rather, we want to help you see how your romantic relationships should prepare you for, and move you towards, the ultimate intimate relationship that God created for romantic and sexual love: marriage. By looking at the high hopes God has for marriage, we can establish high hopes for dating. Dating isn't marriage, and not all dating relationships will or should end in marriage, but we believe that dating done well has value in itself.

However, the behaviours and mindsets that we establish while dating can prepare us for good or bad marriage dynamics. We move towards, or away from, God's high hopes for his wonderful gift of marriage when we begin to date and relate to people intimately. In the next chapter, we're going to begin to unpack some practical advice about dating, but thinking back to our unfinished masterpiece, there are still some aspects of the borders surrounding the picture to which we need to pay attention before we're free to paint the middle of the canvas!

God's marriage mandate

Most people today still have high hopes for marriage, even if they don't see themselves as the marrying type or have had a bad experience. Our friend Chris's parents divorced when he was very young, and he doesn't know too many married couples. But he reckons that one day he would like to get married, and intends to take his vows seriously and remain faithful, come what may.

If dating is the place where we begin to explore some of these expectations for marriage, then it's worth looking at some of the expectations Scripture places on it. It's helpful to keep these in mind when we date, because it will ensure that we establish a godly approach from the very beginning of our search for love. The expectations we see running throughout Scripture can be summed up in the following four categories: Faithfulness is fundamental; seek selflessness; practise permanence; and put God first. As we look at each in turn, our question is always going to be: what does this expectation for marriage teach us about how we should date?

Faithfulness is fundamental

Nothing is more noble, nothing more venerable than fidelity. Faithfulness and truth are the most sacred excellences and endowments of the human mind.
(Marcus Tullius Cicero, 106–43 BC)

There are often mixed messages in popular culture about faithfulness. Have you spotted the way that tabloids handle infidelity? When a relationship breaks down as the result of unfaithfulness, the cheated party is pitied. But the guy or girl trapped in a boring relationship who finds solace elsewhere is congratulated for their courage.

But what does God think?

We're all familiar with the commandment: 'You shall not commit adultery' (Exodus 20:14). You can't get clearer than that! Unfaithfulness, adultery, cheating, or whatever you want to label it, aren't part of God's plan for our relationships. Imagine if your girl/boyfriend cheated on you and then tried to hide it, or worse, didn't even feel guilty about it. The feelings of rejection, broken trust and hurt would be devastating. God calls for faithfulness because he wants us to avoid being hurt, or being the cause of hurt to others.

In Genesis, we not only read about the first marriage, but about God's heart for *all* marriages. In a time when there was no sin in the world, we read about a love story that has faithfulness at its core: faithfulness to God and to each other: 'That is why a man leaves his father and mother and is united to his wife, and they become one flesh' (Genesis 2:24 NIV).

Adam and Eve are 'united' to each other in the same attitude of faithfulness that God wants us to 'unite' with him. It's such a profound union that the only way the Bible writers can adequately explain what has happened is to say that they are no longer two separate beings, but 'one flesh'.

Sometimes we can feel disturbed by the strong language the Bible reserves for unfaithful spouses (check out Deuteronomy 22:22!). But the Bible pulls no punches when it comes to unfaithfulness, because any behaviour that violates this one-flesh union between two people causes damage. It forms part of the Ten Commandments and is unmistakable: 'You must not commit adultery' (Exodus 20:14 NLT).

Cheating causes havoc and is the very opposite of everything God has in mind for relationships. The Old Testament authors realized that God's call for faithfulness came out of his desire for us to enjoy love. He doesn't want us to suffer the negative consequences:

> But a man who commits adultery has no sense;
>> whoever does so destroys himself.
> Blows and disgrace are his lot,
>> and his shame will never be wiped away.
> For jealousy arouses a husband's fury,
>> and he will show no mercy when he takes revenge.
> (Proverbs 6:32–34 NIV)

Jesus, who hardly ever talks about sex, echoes this, classifying unfaithfulness and adultery as evil (Matthew 15:19; Mark 7:21–22). If God's plan for marriage is two people becoming one for life, then anything that compromises this is bad news. The New Testament authors agreed with this whenever the subject arose: the author of Hebrews maintains, 'Give honour to marriage, and remain faithful to one another in marriage. God will surely judge people who are immoral and those who commit adultery' (Hebrews 13:4 NLT).

Whenever we talk about biblical faithfulness and two becoming one, there is a chance that some bright spark might respond with: 'Hang on, there are plenty of men with multiple wives in the Old Testament. Were they being unfaithful?' Well, let's take a brief look at this. While there are stories where much-loved biblical characters have more than one wife at a time (like Jacob in Genesis 29), we need to understand that this wasn't part of God's original design of 'one-flesh' union in marriage. God never tells anyone to marry more than one wife. As you would expect, it always caused trouble and arguments: Sarah drove Hagar away (Genesis 16:4–6; 21:9–11), and sister-wives Rachel and Leah were always at each other's throats (Genesis 29:31 – 30:24). The Bible even says that King Solomon walked away from God because he had multiple wives:

> God had clearly warned Israel, 'You must not marry them . . . '
> Solomon fell in love with them anyway, refusing to give them up.
> He had seven hundred royal wives and three hundred concubines

– a thousand women in all! And they did seduce him away from God. As Solomon grew older, his wives beguiled him with their alien gods and he became unfaithful – he didn't stay true to his God as his father David had done.

(1 Kings 11:1–5 *The Message*)

The Old Testament doesn't reject polygamy outright: instead, it always paints it in a negative light, reminding us that it opposes God's intentions for marriage. These subtle teachings gathered momentum over time, which is why the New Testament authors came to the natural conclusion that church leaders should have one wife: 'The overseer [leader] must be above reproach, the husband of but one wife . . . ' (1 Timothy 3:2 NIV).

But this wasn't just for leaders; everyone had to pay attention: 'Husbands, love your wives, just as Christ loved the church and gave himself up for her to make her holy' (Ephesians 5:25–26 NIV). Love *your* wife, and not other women. Wives deserve love and respect. As obvious as this may sound to us today, it was radical teaching for the time.

God understands the damage that is brought about by unfaithfulness, which is why the Bible speaks so clearly about being committed to *one* person. But people still hurt one another. Even Christians can hurt one another. Some of us might have already experienced the pain of someone cheating on us, or of being in a family devastated by unfaithfulness. God is a loving Father, who can and does restore even the most broken situations. As our good Father, he longs for us to lay different foundations for our future relationships.

So how do we start building some fidelity muscles? Think about what attitudes may lie dormant in you that, if unchecked, could grow into unfaithfulness. Jerry had a hunch that there was always someone better round the corner. He was the only single guy in a church of lots of single women. He never meant to get so emotionally entangled with Esther while he was dating Emma. But he couldn't shake off the idea that maybe he was with the wrong girl. The problem was, he had been with the 'wrong' girl a few times before, and he always started a new relationship with an embarrassing overlap from the previous one.

Focus brings freedom. If we choose to make faithfulness a focus in our lives, we will be free to be in healthy relationships, or see more clearly the unhealthy ones we should walk away from. Let's ask ourselves: does this action or attitude demonstrate faithfulness to this person, or selfishness? What films, music or entertainment am I immersed in that undermine my desire to be faithful? How am I practising faithfulness in my friendships and my family? How have I handled situations where I was the cheater? God is faithful in all his relationships, so by listening to his voice above the other noises, we can start not only to value faithfulness, but to live out his high hopes for us here and now.

Seek selflessness

> Every man [and woman] must decide whether they will walk
> in the creative light of altruism or the darkness of destructive
> selfishness . . . Life's persistent and most urgent question is
> 'What are you doing for others?'
> (Martin Luther King Jr)

In the last chapter we introduced the idea that Christian dating (like every type of relationship we're in) is defined by selflessness. In fact, we can date in a God-glorifying way *only* when we put our girl/boyfriend first. This doesn't only turn everything our culture says about romance on its head; it turns everything ancient culture has said about marriage on its head too!

Paul's comments about marriage were set against the status quo of the day, when women were seen as second-class citizens. But as he wanted to make marriages stronger, so he challenged couples to see each other through God's eyes. The idea that both the husband and wife should consider each other's needs and serve each other must have raised a few eyebrows (check out 1 Corinthians 7:1–6). The real game changer was Paul instructing the husband to love his wife 'just as Christ loved the church and gave himself up for her' (see Ephesians 5:25–33).

These passages don't surprise us today, because we expect people to treat each other well in marriages, but Paul is asking for a lot more than for spouses to tolerate each other. He's asking them to outdo each other in selflessness. Who can give more? Who can show more sacrificial love? It's like a competition! This radical attitude will not only bless their relationship, but it will also be a stunning witness to the ultimate self-giving love of Christ.

Dating built on this understanding of selflessness is bound to create revolutionary relationships. Dating someone who is as committed as you are to demonstrating this kind of love carries the potential for an incredible relationship. Paul would encourage you to seek selflessness, and then seek it again and again and again.

It seems like a very high hope for a new dating relationship, doesn't it? It doesn't happen overnight. Over time, small seeds of selfless acts grow into something beautiful and strong that will lay the foundations for a good, God-focused marriage.

Reflect on dating couples you know who look happy, whom you admire and who seem to be building towards marriage. At the heart of their relationship will be a commitment to take selflessness seriously.

Searching for people who want this too, and dating in a way that is selfless, will help us explore God's hopes for our relationships – and we'll experience the rewards of doing things his way.

Practise permanence

I love being married. It's so great to find that one special person you want to annoy for the rest of your life.
(Rita Rudner)

We live in a culture where the upgrade of four months ago is old news! We want the latest, the freshest, the fastest. Even if it's only a little gadget to add to our blinged-up phone, if it's not the latest, it's not the greatest.

This belief can cause problems for us when it comes to relationships. We know that having a long list of people following or befriending us via social media doesn't constitute deep and meaningful relationships. We all have a deep longing for true belonging. So how does that work in dating relationships, which are often temporary by nature? What would God have to say about the length and depth of our dating?

Dating is not marriage, and it's not a guarantee of permanence. Ending a relationship that doesn't have the potential to evolve into lifelong commitment is not only wise; it's necessary if we're seeking to date in a God-honouring way. So what do we do with the biblical call for lifelong intimate relationships? How do we apply it to a dating context? Did God just get it wrong when he called for *lifelong* faithfulness between people who love each other?

We need to understand why God called for permanence, and why there are times when he made exceptions to this principle. This is the hardest marriage expectation to apply to dating, but we still think it should guide the way we paint our picture. The very first wedding vows ever spoken in the Bible are:

The man said,

> 'This is now bone of my bones
>   and flesh of my flesh;
> she shall be called "woman",
>   for she was taken out of man.'
> (Genesis 2:23 NIV)

See how Adam refers to himself in the third person as 'man', and Eve as 'she' and 'woman', and how he begins with 'This is'.

Adam isn't mumbling to himself or whispering sweet nothings in Eve's ear – he's not that smooth. Rather, he's making his first declaration to someone else; he's talking to the other person in the story: God. Adam calls on God to witness his vow, to witness the permanent fusion between him and Eve. They are now one and the same. God's design for marriage has this hope for permanence built into it. Jesus says,

> Pharisees came up, intending to give him [Jesus] a hard time. They asked, 'Is it legal for a man to divorce his wife?'
>
> Jesus said, 'What did Moses command?'
>
> They answered, 'Moses gave permission to fill out a certificate of dismissal and divorce her.'
>
> Jesus said, 'Moses wrote this command only as a concession to your hardhearted ways. In the original creation, God made male and female to be together. Because of this, a man leaves father and mother, and in marriage he becomes one flesh with a woman – no longer two individuals, but forming a new unity. Because God created this organic union of the two sexes, no one should desecrate his art by cutting them apart.'
>
> (Mark 10:2–9 *The Message*)

Jesus doesn't just look back to the law about divorce (Deuteronomy 24:1–4). He is quoting the Genesis story of creation that reveals God's heart for what relationships free from sin should look like (Genesis 1:27; 2:24). Adam and Eve's later rejection of all this kick-starts the cycle of sin and dysfunction that leads to the damage and pain of marriages wrecked by divorce. As we've said before, relationships and marriages break down for a whole host of reasons, but none of these lessens God's desire for us to really mean it when we say 'I do'!

God realizes that in some cases this permanence can't be maintained, because a spouse can damage it irreversibly. So the Bible allows divorce when a partner commits adultery (Matthew 5:31–32; 19:9), or when an unbelieving spouse abandons their believing spouse (1 Corinthians 7:12–15). We may not be in Eden, but God always hopes for more for us in our relationships. Deep relationships are not easily forged. Intimacy isn't quickly formed. Both take practice and require both people to be committed to permanence. Building towards a relationship that lasts isn't something that happens *in spite* of us; it's something that happens *because* of us. Practising what it takes to build a permanent relationship happens every time we prioritize our commitment over our compulsions. Giving in to every whim and desire we have is no way to perfect the skills needed to build a lasting relationship.

So how could this influence our dating? It's likely that most of us will date a few people before we find the person we want to commit to for life. Does this mean we can't practise permanence? Not if we practise it while we're dating!

It's about the mindset we create as we date. It's the difference between an attitude that says, 'I'll see how it goes', and one that says, 'I'll see what I can invest in this relationship.' Do we go around asking people out, thinking, 'This will only work for me for a few months, and then I'm off'? Do we treat relationships like new clothes, and wear them for only a few weeks before we change? If this is the case, how will we be ready to invest long-term with that special someone when the time comes? If we constantly think short term in every relationship we go into, how is that preparing us for the lifelong commitment God desires?

Put God first

> My only joys therefore are that when God has given me a work to do, I have not refused it.
> (C. T. Studd, missionary to China)

When did you last experience giving God your 'everything'? It could have been during a time of worship at an event, a missions week, or going on a retreat, but that feeling of focusing on God alone made you feel alive. In those times, we wish it could always be this way. Sometimes we can feel jealous or unworthy of the intimacy that 'super-saints' like Moses or David had with God, but this is available to us too. In all times and in all places, we can know an increasing closeness to God.

So what about when we're getting close to the person we're dating? Isn't this the greatest distraction from our focus on God? We often see people struggling to solve the conundrum of how the two work together. You might have friends who had seemed passionately committed to Jesus, and then, within weeks of falling in love, they had lost all interest in anything to do with God. To stop this happening, we might think we need to stop ourselves from dating.

But instead of being the thing that gets in the way of our relationship with God, dating can be about two people working at growing closer to God as they grow closer to each other. This begins with each person putting their thirst for God first.

Scripture shows us that the best way to live starts with putting God first. He comes before our work, our relationships and our pleasure. We are blessed to have a God who wants to give us good things, but we don't put the gifts before the gift giver. He becomes our absolute priority: 'I am the LORD your God, who brought you out of Egypt, out of the land of slavery. You shall have no other gods before me' (Exodus 20:2–3 NIV).

Jesus makes service to God and his will the priority (Luke 9:57–62). Instead of being a restriction, this way of life sets us free to become all we can be.

It won't surprise you, then, that the Bible teaches that the best way to approach marriage is to have God at the centre. Marriage isn't an end in itself, but a way that people can fulfil God's mission together:

> So God created humankind in his own image.
>   In the image of God he created them;
>   male and female he created them.

Then God blessed them and said, 'Be fruitful and multiply. Fill the earth and govern it. Reign over the fish in the sea, the birds in the sky, and all the animals that scurry along the ground.'
(Genesis 1:27–28 NLT)

Marriage should be a place where society sees a couple reflecting God's love for his church as they take their vows seriously (1 Corinthians 6:15–17). God is not deluded; he knows that it's hard to put him first in a marriage. Paul points out that single people don't have the divided loyalties experienced by a married couple (1 Corinthians 7:32–35). This is actually a real advantage of singleness. But Paul isn't anti-marriage; of course it's possible to serve God wholeheartedly and have a spouse and family, but there are more pressures to juggle. It takes work. We are being a bit unrealistic if we think we can date someone and invest all our time and energy in them, neglect our friends, our family and our God, get married, and then instantly begin to put God first.

This is where singleness needs to get a shout-out. We form the habits of serving God before we ever start dating. When we are single, it can be easier to forge a lifestyle that puts God first. Singleness can be lonely, but it's not a waiting room before the real work of a relationship begins. It's an opportunity to seek God, serve him and establish a hunger for building his kingdom – all of which will bless your future dating and married life. It's for these very reasons that some people embrace singleness for life.

Obviously, serving God as a dating couple will look different from serving God as a married couple. It's not wise to change all your life plans after the first date! This is something that will grow over time. But how can you use your relationship to serve God in the opportunities you already have? Tim dated Zoe, a talented musician who was keen to use her musical abilities for God's glory. She loved music therapy and leading worship at her church. Tim didn't know the first thing about music and had little interest in it, but he saw that God had gifted Zoe. So he went along to her music recitals and gave her space and time to practise, instead of demanding that she spend all her time with him. In doing so, he encouraged her to put God's will first. Dating this way requires us to be courageous. It means doing all it takes to chase after God for ourselves and spurring each other on as we chase after him together.

First steps

Faithfulness is fundamental, seek selflessness, practise permanence, and put God first: these are God's high hopes. This is how he wants us to approach the ultimate intimate relationship. If we allow God's goals for our intimate relationships to guide the way we date, then we will find ourselves developing godly behaviours and mindsets that will honour him. We can learn to do this now, instead of waiting until after our wedding day.

Building our hopes for dating on God's expectations for marriage might seem like a tall order – and it is! Dating is not marriage, but we think these principles, along with 'be active' and 'be selfless' can help us to apply God's teaching to our lives.

But we don't bring these ideas to you expecting perfection. We've certainly struggled always to approach our own dating relationships this way. But the alternative is to muddle on, hoping that we're getting it right, and feeling guilty when we get it wrong. That's why we often hope God will give us all the answers up front, rather than realizing that, with godly borders like these to lean on, we can have confidence to think for ourselves and paint an amazing picture.

In one of the most beautiful chapters in the Bible, Paul reminds his readers that failures don't need to have the final say in their lives: 'Therefore, there is now no condemnation for those who are in Christ Jesus' (Romans 8:1 NIV).

Before any of us even consider dating God's way, we need to accept that dating involves broken people. We've talked about releasing other people from being 'the one', which, logically, means that we need to release ourselves from the expectation of being perfect too. None of us is condemned by God for falling short. Every Christian who has ever dated has made mistakes from time to time. Without meaning to, we are all at risk of hurting the people we love, and vice versa. That's why it's so important that we study God's Word and look at where we need to grow, rather than expecting the other person to resolve our issues.

Learning, accepting our faults and asking God to help us change: that's what this revolution is all about.

Chat room

Here are some simple questions for you to reflect on, before we get stuck into our four dating guidelines:

- How have you dated in the past? Are there things you need to repent of to God and to others?
- Do you need to forgive someone for how they have treated you in a previous relationship? Forgiveness is not about letting them off the hook; it's about neutralizing the damage they did to you as you let go of any anger or bitterness towards them.
- In an episode of *New Girl*, a frustrated Jess shouts at Nick, 'You don't have the courage or the patience to be single!' Before you consider who to date well, do you need to spend some time thinking about whether you have been, or are being, single well?
- Do you trust that God wants to bless you, whether you marry someone or not?
- How could you use these four biblical expectations for marriage to help you approach dating?
- How do you feel about the fact that you're not someone's perfect partner? Having a sober view of yourself before God provides the right foundation for building a relationship with someone else who isn't perfect either.

OUR DATING GUIDELINES

At last we've got to the practical bit!

All that has gone before has helped to prepare us to frame dating God's way. Like the artist in chapter 2, we're now ready to fill in the blank part of the canvas and work out how the biblical ideas are applied and expressed in dating.

Love isn't an exact science. Entering a relationship can feel like stepping into the unknown. So our aim is to arm you with as much wisdom as we can in order to help you build your relationship on solid foundations. So whether you're single, dating or waiting, these guidelines are for you.

We've come up with four guidelines: date stronger, date deeper, date clearer and date wider.

Date stronger (chapter 4) is about dating from the best starting point. Looking for someone to date because we feel bored, insecure or incomplete makes our relationships weak right from the start. In this guideline we'll be challenging wrong motives, and finding ways to shift our approach from weakness to strength.

Date deeper (chapter 5) opts for quality over quantity. Daring to go deep means that we need to reject our culture's obsession with shallow, non-committal relationships. In this guideline we'll be exploring how to do this so that we reap the benefits of faithfulness.

Date clearer (chapter 6) looks at who we date. Everyone has unique criteria. The question is: are they the right ones? In this guideline we'll be shining the spotlight not only on what we should look for in our date, but also what they should look for in us.

Date wider (chapter 7) will help you keep your feet on the ground. Nothing can narrow our vision quite like finding our significant other. In this guideline we'll look at how an outward-focused life keeps our dating relationships healthy.

Take your everyday, ordinary life – your sleeping, eating, going-to-work, and walking-around life – and place it before God as an offering. Embracing what God does for you is the best thing you can do for him. Don't become so well-adjusted to your culture that you fit into it without even thinking. Instead, fix your attention on God. You'll be changed from the inside out. Readily recognize what he wants from you, and quickly respond to it. Unlike the culture around you, always dragging you down to its level of immaturity, God brings the best out of you, develops well-formed maturity in you.

(Romans 12:1–2 *The Message*)

CHAPTER FOUR:
DATE STRONGER

My attitude is that if you push me towards something that you think is a weakness, then I will turn that perceived weakness into a strength.
(Michael Jordan, basketball player)

Strength matters

Whether it's emotional, physical or spiritual, the stronger we are, the more we can do. My (André) fiancée's dad decided to power walk the London Marathon a few years ago. Now, by his own admission, he wasn't in the best of shape beforehand. So for the year leading up to the race, he got up at the crack of dawn to run a few miles before work, changed his diet and invested in the correct sports gear too.

He managed to walk the distance in five hours twenty-six minutes and raised over £7,000 for charity! For a marathon runner his time was good, but for a walker who had never done anything like this before in his life, it was incredible!

Another friend also ran a marathon.

Although he wasn't in the best of shape either, he decided not to train beforehand. He didn't change his diet, attempt any mental preparation or put effort into raising money. He finished the marathon – in over twelve hours – but couldn't move the next day. It took him months to recover from the damage he sustained.

Dating someone is different. But there are good lessons to learn from the parable of our two marathon runners. Just as it's a bad idea to run a marathon without first putting in the training, it's a bad idea to start dating without first doing some preparation. We're not talking about a fitness regime or changing our diet. But dating well requires us to work on our core strength. There are a whole load of skills, insights and godly expectations that lay strong foundations for relationships. We'll be exploring them further in this chapter. It's a shame we can't download them the moment we start fancying someone! But even if we could, what would be the point? If our strength comes from within us, we need to put the work in to get ourselves in shape. Failure to do this can result in us either starting relationships we're not ready for, or starting them on weak foundations.

There are some obvious indicators that a relationship has a less-than-secure starting point:

- if you've just met, but both happen to be on a cruise ship that's sinking!
- if one of you is only in it to get citizenship!
- if one or both of you are trying to get back at an ex!

But how about knowing whether we're even ready to date? And why? There are going to be times when it's clearly not a good idea to start:

- if you're uncertain about yourself and need some time to discover who you are

- if you're still reeling from a painful relationship and need some healing time
- if you're convinced that the incompleteness you feel will be fixed by the next person you date

Life on hold

Do you remember the 'You complete me' line from *Jerry Maguire*? Even though this film is quite old now, it resonates with a longing within us that one day we will meet that person who will complete us. We might not even realize we think like this. But believing that we'll be complete when someone gives their heart to us is a bit like thinking that, when the pistol goes off, our bodies will instantly be in the right shape to run a marathon.

All of us have insecurities that we feel need to be hidden away from others. Knowing that we have flaws can make us feel unworthy of love, or insecure about being in a relationship, even if we're longing for it. Probably all of us approach relationships from this starting point, because none of us is perfect.

If we don't have this kind of self-awareness, we might be heading for a rude wake-up call! So if we accept that we're less than perfect when we start relationships, what do we need to work on? Surely we're not expected to go through a Dating Academy before we're allowed to start a relationship?

Of course not! But we need to own up to some home truths. How many of us want to be in a relationship in order to make the loneliness disappear? How many of us are planning our lives around finding someone? How many of us are holding back, living half a life, hoping that, when he or she comes along, we'll finally get to live the whole life we've always dreamed of? It doesn't have to be this way.

An intimate relationship does not banish loneliness. Only when we are comfortable with who we are can we truly function

independently in a healthy way, can we truly function within a relationship. Two halves do not make a whole when it comes to a healthy relationship: it takes two wholes.
(Patricia Fry)

Dating isn't about finding our other half to complete us. It's about building a relationship built on two people sharing two full lives. Waiting around for that leggy blonde or tall handsome stranger to make us whole and strong will keep us passive and weak. We might be unaware of it, but by playing this waiting game, we're also demonstrating selfishness. Expecting someone to do the work of completing us absolves us of taking the responsibility to do it ourselves.

It also ignores the fact that only one person has the power to make us whole.

God is waiting for us to surrender our life to him. He doesn't take control from us; instead he invites us to say 'yes' to the work of his Spirit in shaping our character to be more like his Son, Jesus. Building our security and identity on Jesus gives us the strongest foundation for any relationship. Whether we're single or dating, knowing that we have our feet firmly placed on the rock, Jesus, enables us to start dating well. In our experience, when we begin to do this, God begins to shift our perspective away from our insecurities and fears, and towards his vision for our lives.

> I don't want a relationship that holds me back; I want one that will cause me and him to do more for God.
> (Sarah)

We've broken this guideline up into four practical steps that will help us 'be active' and 'be selfless' as we date. As you engage with them, invite God's Spirit to be with you, provoking you in areas of your life where he wants to make you stronger.

1. Check it out!

Before we can date from a position of strength, we need to think about what holds us back and weakens our relationships. A good starting point is to consider our expectations – we all have a mixture of healthy and unhealthy ones. Here is a list of questions to get you thinking whether your expectations are keeping your life on hold, or setting you up for a healthy relationship:

1. *Do I date because everyone else is dating?* (Hidden expectation: I want this relationship to help me get peer approval.)
2. *Do I date because I feel lonely?* (Hidden expectation: this relationship must fill the emptiness I feel.)
3. *Do I date because I don't value my uniqueness?* (Hidden expectation: this relationship will help me to like myself.)
4. *Do I date because I think it will sort out some of my problems?* (Hidden expectation: this relationship will make the pain and fear go away.)
5. *Do I date because I want to be loved?* (Hidden expectation: this relationship will complete me.)
6. *Do I date because I am bored?* (Hidden expectation: this relationship will entertain me.)
7. *Do I date because the opportunity arose?* (Hidden expectation: this relationship will sort itself out.)

Answering 'yes' to any of these doesn't make us a bad person to be in a relationship with, but we can't just leave things there. It's important to address our unrealistic expectations, because, if they go unchecked, they will hold us back.

I (Rachel) used to expect unrealistic levels of trust and commitment in any new relationship, so I would worry if I didn't have very deep and meaningful conversations with my boyfriend on a daily basis. I expected the relationship to make my fears go away. I remember one relationship finishing when a boyfriend who challenged me on this received a very over-the-top defensive reaction.

A year after the relationship had ended, a good friend spoke and prayed with me, helping me see how my constant need for reassurance from someone I was dating drove even the nicest guys away! It was hard to hear, but it helped me to change my unrealistic expectations and allowed my heart to grow. If I had learned this earlier, I could have been kind to my boyfriend by letting him know of my hopes and fears, and together we could have done something about it.

Here's our list of unhealthy expectations:

Unrealistic expectations for a dating relationship

We will meet all of each other's needs.

They will know what I'm thinking or feeling without me having to say (and vice versa).

They will never want to discuss feelings or talk about the future.

We will spend all our time together.

We will agree on everything.

They will earn a certain amount of money or have a certain status.

I will not budge from my ideals of how they should look.

They will never challenge me.

They will always make me feel happy.

We will immediately know that we belong together, so we will definitely get married.

They will fit into my life.

They will always do what I say.

I will not have to change, but they will change for me.

They will be stronger in their faith, so they will always know what to do.

I will only date the person I know God has told me to marry.

It will be easy.

Having expectations is not a bad thing. Having no expectations at all would be disastrous! Rather, consider how you could adopt these good expectations:

Realistic expectations of a dating relationship

We will have fun together.
We will be open with each other and grow in trust and commitment.
I will remain true to myself as I seek to change for the better.
We will work through disagreements.
We will have a similar view of relationships.
Sometimes we will need some space, but we will always try to communicate well.
We will share core beliefs and values, and enjoy debating areas where we differ.
We will seek to bring out the best in each other.
We will consider each other's needs.
We will spend time apart.
We will encourage each other.
We will not gossip about each other to our friends.
I will still nurture my own relationship with Jesus.
We will share a connection that we will want to nurture into something more.
We will be open to God speaking to us, together and individually, about our relationship.

The thing about our expectations is that they can be hugely influential in governing how we act around someone. Choosing healthy expectations will make your relationship stronger, because it will focus your attention on all the right things and also help you set the right goals. The danger is that, in setting unrealistic expectations, the relationship can often be doomed to fail from the start.

In the past, I (André) thought that, once I starting dating a girl, she would want to do what I wanted! When I wanted to rest, she would sit there and relax; when I wanted to go out, she would be ready and waiting. I thought it would be easy. But I soon realized that things aren't that simple, that I needed to do things I didn't want to do. Like having a chat because she wants to communicate when I'm feeling tired, or going out to something I don't enjoy. I had to change my mindset and approach the relationship with realistic expectations, and learn to support, encourage and communicate – even when I was tired and grumpy.

We need to be active and challenge our own unrealistic expectations. This helps us to shift from a position of weakness to one of strength. So what expectations are making you weak? What could you replace them with?

2. Fill up!

You are unique.

Do you ever think about that? One way to strengthen yourself before dating well is to get to know yourself well. What are you into? What fulfils you? What activities or interests feed your soul and make you feel alive? What stretches you intellectually, physically, emotionally, socially?

Where are your God-given uniqueness and potential being expressed?

This is a brilliant way of making sure your whole life isn't about the next big relationship. Invest in loving your life, now. A friend of ours once said,

> Most women in my church are not asking God about
> their calling or doing much, because they are waiting for
> a husband. He will decide what they do. I think it's a
> shame.
> (Jenny)

Your life is already happening, and there's so much for you to discover about yourself. Try stepping out of your comfort zone: do something for others, like serving in church or volunteering in a community project. You'll experience a deeper sense of fulfilment. The more you appreciate the personality and gifts God has given you, the more confident you will be in sharing who you are in a relationship, without needing the other person to fulfil you. Loving yourself more is a positive effect of being in a good relationship, but it isn't a good *reason* for wanting a relationship. All of us have days where we're not big fans of ourselves, but if you struggle to really see what someone else could ever see in you, find someone you trust to talk it through with. This doesn't make you weak – quite the opposite! It makes you intentional and active.

At the core of growing stronger is knowing that God's opinion of us is enough. Have you noticed how it can be so easy to tell others that God loves them, but so hard to believe it for yourself? We have a God who loves us unconditionally and calls us his children (Galatians 3:26 – 4:7) and his friends (John 15:12–15). This means that we are always somebody worth getting to know. He never regretted making us:

> I praise you, for I am fearfully and wonderfully made.
>   Wonderful are your works.
> (Psalm 139:14 NRSV)

The psalmist is confident that God knows and rejoices in our specially designed lives. Jesus said that he alone brings life to the full (John 10:10). God is the ultimate source of our identity and self-esteem, and in his generosity he has made us as social creatures, hungry for vast interaction with people, ideas and adventures. Investing in good and varied friendships, and developing your mind and interests, are all part of growing strong and preparing yourself for life and love.

If you're currently single, you have a fantastic opportunity to embrace who you are now. Choosing to invest in your life and future doesn't mean that you're shutting the door on ever finding someone. It means you are being active and seeking God's potential for your life. By doing this now, you're giving yourself a head start.

For some of us this process may take a while. I (André) had to choose to be single and purposefully not seek a relationship for a long while, so that I could get my head around who I was and who God was calling me to become. It wasn't easy, but I'm so glad I invested in myself in this way before I met Becca. God was with me the whole time and taught me a lot about myself. I discovered that singleness is a time to grow strong.

If you're already dating, investing in yourself doesn't mean that you're being selfish in your relationship. By giving each other the space to do things with other people (as well as together), it will enable your hearts and relationship to grow.

So what are you going to do? What looks fun to you? What ministry in your church needs more volunteers? Do things that look new or stretch you in different ways. See what happens when you tap into your God-given potential.

3. Stop obsessing!

Have you ever felt so desperate to make a good impression on someone that you've found yourself acting a bit odd around them? Falling for someone has a habit of making fools out of us all. But there's a more serious consequence to this pitfall. Obsessing about finding a relationship or being with a certain person takes up head space and energy. It distracts us from finding fulfilment elsewhere. We pin all our hopes on one person and we can begin to compromise who we are, to lose sight of what God has called us to. This weakens us and any relationship we start, because no-one can fulfil us to that degree.

So how do we date without obsessing? Before we answer that, see if you recognize yourself in any of the following:

You long for a relationship so much that you'll go out with
    anyone.
You never talk with God about your relationships or ask
    him to guide you.
You never talk with God about anything except your
    relationships and future girl/boyfriend.
Now you're dating, everything is about them.
You dismiss singleness as 'God's waiting room'.

The chances are we're probably all guilty of some of these
things. We have all made our search for love an idol at some
point. If you're obsessing about someone you're not yet dating,
the *worst* thing you can do is start going out with them! You may
well be great for each other in the future, but right now you are
about to build a weak relationship because you are asking them
to be everything they can't be. When we find ourselves obsessing
about someone to the point where it's taking over, we need to
bring it to God. A friend told us:

> When I'm in a relationship I often ignore God. I lose sight of the
> bigger picture. If it was the other way round and I ignored my
> boyfriend this much, I would get dumped!
> (Hannah)

She realized she needed to change, and that was the beginning
of things shifting for her. It may also mean that you need to
take control of your thoughts and distract yourself, not in a 'I'll-
avoid-the-issue' kind of way, but rather in a 'I'll-stop-sitting-
here-wallowing-in-my-obsession' way. Go out with other friends,
or spend evenings on your own, reminding yourself that you are
a complete person, with or without someone to date.

    Many bad decisions are made in haste, so often the best thing
to do is to wait. If you fancy someone in March and still feel a
connection in May, then perhaps there is something there. If you
fancy someone at 9 am but have gone off them by 9 pm, it's

probably best to leave them alone! Imagine how unkind and self-centred it would be to put someone on a pedestal, date them and then drop them – all because they had the audacity not to match up to the crazy ideal you had of them in the first place. You could even spend time away from them and chat to some wise friends about your feelings, to see if it's right to continue. We can sometimes obsess about our friendships too. Recognizing if this is our weakness will help us do something about it.

Being free from romantic obsessions means we don't need to:

- make them the reason for our existence
- put our life on hold until they show up
- be afraid to face the truth of how unhealthy this (potential) relationship is

This is all part of becoming the selfless boy/girlfriend that God calls us to be. It will make us and our relationships stronger.

4. Be quiet!

Have you ever been out with someone who talks about themselves continually? It's a real turn-off, isn't it? Or have you ever fancied someone who thinks they're all that? You may like them to begin with, but after a while you just want to get away. There's nothing uglier than self-centredness.

But we're constantly being told to make ourselves the lord of our own universe. How do you feel about the number of friends you have on Facebook? How desperate are you to increase your number of Twitter followers? Yep, self-absorption shows us up in all sorts of ways.

The final step in this guideline challenges us to get our egos out of the way so that we can date well.

When Jesus becomes Lord of our lives, a change of power takes place, and although painful at times, it's for our own good. Paul instructs us to take off our old self and focus on God and his ways

(Ephesians 4:22–24). We don't need to make our mark, stamp our authority or demand that someone notices or listens to us in order to know that we're somebody. It's the same when we're dating. If we fill every silence with the latest story that makes us look good, then we're not allowing space for the other person to share their thoughts and feelings. A sign of a good relationship is that you both feel accepted for who you are, not for what you say or the good times you can generate. If one of you demands that everything is about you all the time (*your* thoughts, *your* problems, *your* funny stories), then you might find the other person feels there's no room for them in your life. It's already crowded with you!

One of our friends really fancied a girl and thought she was amazing. But once she opened her mouth, he quickly discovered just how self-absorbed she was; everything was about her. His feelings of attraction faded quickly. He recognized the power in talking and listening to one another, discussing things beyond their own worlds. Her inability to give, rather than just take, was not only annoying; it was ugly.

Think about people you respect deeply: our guess is they don't obsess about themselves all the time. They have a beautiful ability to reach out to others and give of themselves.

So here's a challenge for you. Why not let your girlfriend, boyfriend or friend do the talking? Listen to them. Really listen to them!

But don't stop there. Who else could you reach out to? Ask God to give you more compassion for someone you know who is struggling. Take someone out to dinner or the cinema and pay for it. Offer to do something more costly for someone. Stretch your faith. Putting others first doesn't come easily, but it revolutionizes our dating.

A whole life

Dating from a position of strength will help us to apply God's desire for us to be selfless and active. Reflecting on our expectations, seeking a full and well-rounded life, avoiding obsession and learning to put others first will give us the strength we need. It will allow us to date with a full life that we can share, rather than waiting for someone to fix us.

Chat room

- What hobbies/activities excite you? What are you going to invest in?
- What activity at church or in the community could you volunteer for to serve others?
- How much time do you make for your friends, family, workmates, neighbours?
- Be honest with yourself about the amount of time you spend thinking or obsessing about your (future) girl/boyfriend?
- If you fancy someone, how are you going to make space so that you can think about it with a clear head?
- How can you be more patient?
- Have you found yourself putting your life on hold for this new relationship – even in subtle ways? What can you do to make some changes?
- Do you know what God's purpose is for your life? Do you have someone you can chat and pray this through with?
- Whose perspective on your relationships do you most seek and trust?
- What are you like at listening to other people?
- Do you allow anyone in your life to challenge you on unhealthy attitudes or behaviour when it comes to relationships? If not, why not? And who could you ask to help you break some unhealthy patterns?
- Are there any aspects of your current/previous relationship that you feel unhappy about and want to make sure you change/don't repeat? Who could help you identify these? How will you make the right changes?

CHAPTER FIVE:
DATE DEEPER

We have to recognise that there cannot be relationships unless there is commitment, unless there is loyalty, unless there is love, patience, persistence.
(Cornel West)[16]

Nearly, but not yet

Films are full of 'nearly-but-not-yet' moments. It's that point where the main character is about to get everything they ever wanted (generally the love of their life), but hesitates and then can't decide if it's what they really wanted after all. The grass is always greener and all that. Invariably there is a montage full of tears (if the protagonist is female) or punching walls (if the protagonist is male), before the inevitable conclusion is reached and they can start their happy ever after. Cue long on-screen kiss, credits and we all head home.

But what happens next?

If the two characters existed in real life, what *would* happen next? Would they keep the same level of happiness they had enjoyed in the last scene? Would they never argue, never stray? Would the bad behaviour that propelled the plot line *not* rear its ugly head again?

But how often do you see sequels where the hard-won relationship of the first film is still intact? Relationships don't last long in Hollywood. The films show us how to find 'love', but they cannot teach us how to keep it. In the film *The Hangover*, the groom, late for his own wedding, makes a chivalrous promise to his fiancée: 'I promise, for as long as we're married, I'll never ever put you through anything like this again.' But wait a minute, he didn't say, 'for the rest of my life', or 'until we die'; he only said, 'as long as we are married'.

Imagine marrying someone who thinks there's a good chance they will not be with you for long. Would that be the best day of your life? Obviously, we can't see the future. Many would say that there is always a chance of divorce in any marriage. But to go in with that mindset will surely destroy the relationship.

That's marriage, but what about dating relationships? Could the same rule apply? Imagine dating someone who is also keeping their options open, in case someone 'better' comes along. Or is chasing lots of people, just to see which one of you says yes? Nick started 'seeing' someone he met via a Christian dating website. They really clicked, so they arranged to meet. Over coffee they chatted about lots of things: life experiences, jobs, future hopes, football teams and so on. Then she delivered the killer blow: 'I'm meeting a few guys at the moment, keeping my options open. Hopefully it will work out with someone.'

He felt used.

Remember, earlier we saw God's expectations for marriage, how he asks his people to be faithful and build permanent relationships? The way we date should foster these ideals. If we date in a way that involves cheating, waiting for someone better, or going in with no intention of making it work long-term, then we're not following God's design. We need to be deeply committed people, rather than shallow.

> Commit your way to the LORD;
>> trust in him and he will do this:
> he will make your righteous reward shine like the dawn,
>> your vindication like the noonday sun.
>
> (Psalm 37:5–6 NIV)

Nick felt used by someone who wasn't practising God's expectations for her dating life. Although she valued faithfulness in her friendships and relationship with God, she didn't see how this should affect how she dated. In doing so, she missed a profound truth: we all crave faithfulness in all our relationships, because God created us with this hunger. Faithfulness in marriage starts by practising faithfulness when we're *not* married. So when it comes to dating, what should practising faithfulness look like? When should you commit exclusively to date only him or her: After an email? After the first date? After you're engaged? How do we value fidelity and permanence when the start of a new relationship is delicate? How do we date deeply?

Take Kerry and Tom. A mutual friend suggested they should meet. So they made contact with each other and had a great first date over coffee. Kerry immediately warmed to Tom's attentiveness and humour. Tom liked Kerry's laugh and passion for life. So they arranged the next date. It wasn't so great; Kerry was tired from work, and Tom felt distracted by the pressures of his new job. But all was not lost; they were mature enough to realize that you can't judge people on only two dates. So they met again, and this time everything was wonderful. During the conversation, Tom slipped in his appreciation of strong women, but also that he likes to be the protective guy in a relationship and make the moves.

So Kerry went home and waited for Tom to make the next move.

She waited and waited and waited. She dropped him a couple of warm and funny texts. No reply. Weeks went by. Months went by. Having been hurt by a long-term relationship that had ended badly, Kerry was keen not to hang around, waiting to see if Tom was going to come back into her life.

There may have been really good reasons why Tom didn't get in touch. But if we are truly to date God's way, we can't leave people in any doubt as to whether or not we want to meet up again, and we certainly shouldn't keep them hanging on. Treating exclusivity as something we may or may not do, depending on how we feel, leaves people wondering what we're about. It's selfish behaviour that doesn't take faithfulness seriously, hurts others and lays weak foundations for a relationship.

Love triangles

Lots of churches struggle with having only a few single people around the same age. There's always the possibility that we might end up dating someone's ex, or their future spouse! People sometimes refer to this as a love triangle. In all honesty, churches often have love triangles mixed with love squares, love trapeziums, love octagons, love tetrahedrons: there are more shapes in church than in a maths textbook! It can be hard to keep up sometimes. Inevitably, this puts real strain on new relationships and existing friendships.

Because of this, some couples choose to keep their love a secret. We've known couples who have conducted 'stealth' relationships and gone to considerable lengths to keep people in the dark. But friendships depend on a level of openness and honesty. Secrecy isn't the best way for us to demonstrate faithfulness to our boy/girlfriend or our friendship groups.

If you or your date have a relationship history, it's important that you're honest with yourselves and others about being in a new relationship. Keeping it a secret for fear of upsetting your ex doesn't honour them. Instead, treat them with dignity; don't ignore them. Don't ask friends to choose between you and them. Also, secrecy isn't a great foundation for a new relationship. Instead, a healthy way to respect your ex's feelings is to conduct your relationship sensitively in public. That means not talking about your new relationship all the time and being seen without each other at events, as well as together, so that you continue to invest in friendships and your well-rounded life.

As difficult as it sounds, a past relationship has to be just that – a past relationship. If your past relationships are still very present in your life, because your friendships overlap, or Twitter and Facebook updates and messages keep popping up, then you need to make sure that you aren't encouraging or seeking emotional intimacy from them. Your priority is to invest in your new relationship. Your ex also needs to be free for a new relationship that they might not pursue if they are still getting some of their needs met by you.

Juliet knew that Matthew was so in love with her that even remaining 'friends' would be too difficult for him. When she gently told him that she was going to delete his number and not contact him for a while, he was devastated and told her it felt like being dumped all over again. So she relented. But as she predicted, every time they met 'just as friends', he would end up pouring out his heart to her, only to be rejected all over again when she said she didn't feel for him in that way. After a very late-night phone chat, he angrily agreed that they shouldn't meet up again. Juliet was relieved, then desperately sad at how much pain she had caused Matthew. It took lots of chats with good friends for her to realize that it was *because* she cared for him as a friend that she wanted to release him from the hope of them dating again.

They bumped into each other a year later, and although it was a bit awkward, both of them knew they had done the right thing.

As we are all unique, we will handle past relationships differently. Choosing to stay in touch 'just as friends' might work for *you*, but make sure that it's working for *both* of you. If it does, great! Jason and I (Rachel) have stayed in touch with one of my boyfriends. In fact, he's become one of Jason's closest friends. But there was a gap of a few years between this guy breaking my heart and becoming my husband's buddy!

You might be in the position of being the 'previous relationship', or maybe you fancied someone who rejected you, and you're finding it hard to move on. It can be especially hard if this person is still meeting some of your emotional needs. Be kind to yourself and focus on what you really need. Even if you feel, or have been told, that you are someone's second choice, you can still choose whether or not to live by that.

Although you're anxious about what life without them will be like, all the time you're holding on to the past, thinking that you can't cope without them. So you're missing out on the healing and rebuilding process that God's Spirit *will* do in your life. Learning to lean on him will enable you to keep tapping into the potential he has given you.

Delving deep

To help us think about what dating deeper looks like, we've come up with four steps. For some of us, the idea of committing to someone and being exclusive and faithful feels daunting. Others may feel that it's something good for the future, but isn't for now, because you don't want to tie yourself down to someone. We're going to challenge both of these misconceptions!

Nate had a girlfriend he was really into, but he was scared to commit to her in case he got hurt or missed out on a better relationship. A close friend challenged him to think about why his relationship with Jesus is so significant to him. 'Is it,' his friend asked, 'the thrill of not knowing whether Jesus will love you tomorrow that keeps things alive? Or is it the fact that you know God loves you, no matter what, and will always accept you, sparing nothing, even his own Son? Do you have a problem with him wanting a deep relationship with you?'

We need to realize that God's way of relating to us is deep, and it's only when we emulate this with those around us that we are able to overcome past hurts and pursue more meaningful relationships with others.

> The steadfast love of the LORD never ceases,
>> his mercies never come to an end;
> they are new every morning;
>> great is your faithfulness.
> (Lamentations 3:22–23 NRSV)

> For I am convinced that neither death, nor life, nor angels, nor rulers, nor things present, nor things to come, nor powers, nor height, nor depth, nor anything else in all creation, will be able to separate us from the love of God in Christ Jesus our Lord.
> (Romans 8:38–39 NRSV)

1. If you want to go deep, be exclusive

Imagine a genie gave you the choice of being fluent in one other language or being able to say 'great to meet you' in every language on the planet. Which would you choose? It would be impressive to be able to say one thing in every language, but in the end, where would it get us? Nice party piece, but it won't change our lives. Yet being fluent in another language would mean that we could visit that country, perhaps get a job and immerse ourselves in the culture. Going deep into one language would be potentially life-changing. Going deep into one relationship is the same.

If we want to be deep, we need to think about what makes us shallow. What traps do we fall into without even realizing it?

1. How many of your 'friends' on Facebook are your actual friends?

2. When did you last meet with friends and both switch your gadgets off in order to concentrate fully on being in the moment together?
3. How often do you spend time alone, in the company of your own thoughts, without noise from the TV or music?
4. If you had a day to yourself, what would you do?
5. Do you know any of the people who live in your house, street or community?
6. How often do you think about the needs of others? Compare that with how often you think about your own needs.
7. When was the last time you spoke to someone for the sake of it, without wanting something in return?

Spending quality time with people we love requires exclusivity. We can't be texting people or taking calls if we want them to feel valued by us. The Bible constantly encourages us to live deep lives by being mindful of others. It celebrates committed and loyal friendships where the friend comes first, like David and Jonathan in 1 Samuel, and Ruth and Naomi in the book of Ruth. Ecclesiastes 4:9–10 says,

> It's better to have a partner than go it alone.
> Share the work, share the wealth.
> And if one falls down, the other helps,
> But if there's no one to help, tough!
> (*The Message*)

Before you start seeing someone, it's possible to demonstrate a level of exclusivity that will build a good foundation. As you read this, some of you are probably thinking this is a bit extreme. It's not like you've said vows in front of a vicar. The person you fancy may not even like you and may be pursuing someone else. But we're not saying that, if you ever fancy someone, you have to ask them out and gear yourselves up to get married!

What we are encouraging you to do is to start as you mean to go on. If you're planning on building a boat, why begin by sticking up tent poles? If you're planning on building a happy relationship, it's got to be a committed one. It's only when we know that the person we're with is not seeing anyone else that we feel safe enough to open up and share our lives. We all want this, so let's start as we mean to go on. After sharing a bit about yourselves, you may discover you're not right for each other, you may break up. But starting deeply will give you that insight early on.

So here are some of our top tips to help you start reaping the benefits of being exclusive:

1. *Watch the flirting.* If you're about to start a new relationship, or you fancy someone, don't flirt with other people. Going after several people doesn't signal a desire for commitment. Flirting and being friendly are not the same thing, but if you're in doubt, ask a friend to give you some honest feedback about whether your friendliness might be leading someone on.

2. *Be ready to put in the work.* So many new relationships start and then burn out just as quickly because one or both of you hadn't considered whether you have time to invest in a relationship. Being committed means being prepared to give this new relationship space and room to grow. We can't just fall into relationships without thinking.

3. *Stop shopping.* Don't worry, we don't mean literal shopping, but once you have found someone who you are keen to date, stop looking around for someone 'better'!

4. *End it early.* If you've been investing time in getting to know each other and then discover that you're not right together, it's better to end the relationship earlier. Dragging out a relationship that is slowly dying makes it too easy for you to start looking for someone else before you're free to do so.

5. *Don't give up.* Sometimes relationships end against our will. This can be really painful. Pursuing love comes with a fair number of disappointments. It doesn't mean that, if it doesn't work out with that person, you will never find love.

6. *Be wise.* Remember, our commitment to being exclusive doesn't mean we are to stay trapped in a relationship that's abusive or damaging. Choosing God's best for us sometimes means walking away from someone if we are not able to be in a healthy relationship with them.

In case all of this commitment talk is putting you off asking someone out because it feels way too serious, relax! Forming a new relationship is supposed to be enjoyable, because it's full of lots of exciting firsts: the first time you have a deep and meaningful chat, the first time you pray together, the first time you refer to each other as your boy/girlfriend, the first time you hold hands, the first blazing row, the first kiss. But it's at the very moment that we want to be going full speed ahead that we need to learn to pace ourselves!

2. Go deep, don't sink!

Getting to know someone can be intoxicating and incredible. You share thoughts that no-one else knows and feel alive when you're near them. This is intimacy. It grows through a number of levels. Barbara Wilson outlines these in her book, *The Five Levels of Intimacy.*

> *Level one:* When we start liking someone we want to get to know them. 'Chatting someone up' is simply a way of building a link with someone through conversation.
>
> *Level two:* We get to know a bit about the person we're attracted to: their values and beliefs. Things are getting more personal as we're making choices about whether this person's values match ours or not.

Level three: We feel safe to share our values and beliefs with them. This opens us up to the possibility of rejection, and this is where relationships between Christians and non-Christians often end.

Level four: We share our feelings and experiences by talking about our mistakes, hopes and dreams. Have you ever started talking at this level with someone too soon? You probably felt a bit vulnerable, especially if they're not doing the same.

Level five: We explore each other's deepest needs, desires and emotions. It's at this level that we open ourselves up to the greatest experience any relationship can ever offer, and the greatest risk of rejection. So we save this for marriage: that ultimate commitment that alone makes us safe enough to give ourselves completely to the other person.[17]

As you prepare to go deep in your dating relationship, consider how you can travel together emotionally. Be careful that you don't jump into intimate conversations before you have established the foundations, trusting each other and feeling safe with who they are as a person.

Exclusivity is good, but we must remember that *intimacy* takes time to grow.

So alongside being exclusive, we need to be wise in how we nurture intimacy. Rushing headlong into vulnerability and pinning all our hopes on one person can be overwhelming for them. Exclusivity doesn't mean intensity. Our trust and intimacy with each other need to flourish over time. As you commit yourself to being exclusive and going deep, avoid sinking into intimacy that you're not yet ready for. We had a friend who went out with a girl, and by the second week she was already planning their wedding and life together. She was opening her heart up as if they had been going out for years. They say that fools rush in. So be wise and protect your heart. Let love grow.

Do not arouse or awaken love
until it so desires.
(Song of Solomon 8:4 NIV)

3. Looking at your boy/girl, only

So you've found someone, you're growing together slowly, but you have this niggling suspicion that there might be someone better for you out there. But wait a minute, we wouldn't want our girl/boyfriend to be waiting for someone better than us to come along, would we? If that's not how we want to be seen, why do we allow ourselves to do it to others? Everyone would accept that, if we went and kissed someone else, it would be cheating. But being faithful is more than physical stuff. Dating deeper challenges us to let our faithfulness run deep, affecting what we think as well as how we act.

> I think I would feel more hurt and more betrayed if I found out that my future husband was having meaningful conversations and sharing secrets with another woman than if he had slept with someone else.
> (Keri)

So what do you think about flirting or having deep and meaningful chats with someone of the opposite sex? Is it OK to look but not touch? Even if it is 'innocent', this kind of behaviour might still make our boy/girlfriend feel inadequate. Deciding whether or not we should do something isn't just about what we feel happy with; it's also about the impact it has on the person we love and would do anything for. God wants relationships to be marked with selflessness.

It can be difficult to stop our wandering eyes. For us lads, it can sometimes feel like we are hardwired to look at as many girls as possible. With our culture's focus on sex, more and more girls are struggling as well. So how do we avoid doing this when for most of us it will be a constant battle? For me (André), lust is always something I'm battling against. We all need God's grace.

There are two things we can do. First, remember we always have a choice. If we're walking down the street and see a gorgeous man/woman and are attracted to them, that's OK; it's a natural reaction. However, if we keep looking, or look away and look back again, then we're feeding the lust and it will grow. If you want to conquer your lust, don't fuel it by feeding it. Kill it by starving it! The first look is a reaction; the second look is a choice. Dating someone doesn't mean we won't be attracted to anyone else, but dating someone well means choosing to starve our appetite for what we can't have.

Secondly, we need to stop filling our heads with pictures of sex. Carrying porn – pictures or videos – around on our phones won't help. Listening to music with sexually explicit lyrics and engaging in sexual banter with friends make unfaithfulness seem normal, and will cause us to be constantly distracted by sex and to read overtly sexual messages into situations. Remember, our will-power is not enough on its own. We need God's Spirit, which is readily available. Right here, right now.

Flirting is another pitfall, because it can so easily be misunderstood. We probably all need to be challenged about this from time to time. Only having eyes for the person we're dating also means having our ears open to what they're saying! Sometimes they may overreact, but we need to be sensitive and humble. We might not think that a meaningful conversation with someone late at night is flirting, but it may look like it to the person we're dating. We need to balance the intimacy that we foster with other people, so that it's not a threat to our relationship.

Seeing faithfulness in this broad way might be new to some of us. But whether or not we've considered it in that way before, it's still a huge challenge. We probably all know of relationships that have ended because there was physical unfaithfulness. But how many have ended because someone was tempted to look elsewhere?

True happiness . . . is not attained through self-gratification, but through fidelity to a worthy purpose.
(Helen Keller)

So if you're single or in a relationship, how will you nurture exclusivity? Ask yourself: is there anything I'm filling my life with that undermines God's gift of faithfulness? How am I exercising self-control when I see an attractive person? Am I off balance in the way I share myself in any intimate relationships?

4. Not looking back in anger

Have you noticed how even the best-laid plans don't always work out?

Sometimes even healthy dating relationships end, and others that look promising never get off the ground. We need to be careful that we don't let these experiences make us resentful towards God or others. A bad experience is not a reason to throw all of our values and intentions out of the window. Dating deep is worthwhile, even if it doesn't turn out as we had hoped. Pursuing one person and committing to them exclusively is always the best way to date. Not because that's what we say, but because we have seen that's how God has designed it.

I love you, LORD, my strength.
The LORD is my rock, my fortress and my deliverer;
   my God is my rock, in whom I take refuge,
   my shield and the horn of my salvation, my stronghold.
I called to the LORD, who is worthy of praise,
   and I have been saved from my enemies.
The cords of death entangled me;
   the torrents of destruction overwhelmed me.
The cords of the grave coiled around me;
   the snares of death confronted me.
In my distress I called to the LORD;
   I cried to my God for help.

From his temple he heard my voice;
    my cry came before him, into his ears.
(Psalm 18:1–6 NIV)

What an amazing psalm! When our hopes, dreams and plans don't go according to plan, God's deep constancy provides us with hope and security that we can rely on. His promises aren't empty.

The LORD is my rock, my fortress and my deliverer;
    my God is my rock, in whom I take refuge.

Keep the faith

Dating deeply challenges us to build a relationship with one person at a time, demonstrate faithfulness even before we go out, and realize that being faithful includes our intentions and thoughts, as well as our actions. We've probably all hurt others, or been hurt, in relationships. Knowing God and choosing to date in a way that honours him won't necessarily prevent this from happening again. But the reason we keep choosing to date deeply is because the lifelong love we want is found only through faithfulness. Loving deeply will open us up to the possibility of being rejected. Dating God's way doesn't come with any guarantees! But even when hurt happens, we can know the healing power of Jesus and find the courage to date deeply again.

Chat room

- Reflect on how much God is committed to you, how deeply he loves you and cares for you. How can you deepen your relationship with him?
- What can you do to deepen your relationships with your friends and family?

- Do your thoughts demonstrate someone who is ready to commit? Are you ready to be with just one person?
- Do you find that you fancy more than one person at a time?
- Are you aware of the negative impact that certain things you watch or listen to can have on your attitude to faithfulness?
- Do you look at pornography? Do you think it nurtures faithfulness and commitment? (See Appendix 1, p. 209.)
- Is there a romantic situation you need to step back from (like feeling torn between two people you're attracted to)?
- Do you suffer from sexual distractedness? Are you constantly looking for the next 'hottie' to walk by, or the chance to make a sexual innuendo? What do you want to do about it?
- Do you need to forgive those who have damaged you in past relationships, causing you to put up barriers to avoid committing to people?
- How can you allow intimacy to grow slowly?
- How can you be more exclusive emotionally?
- Do you need to ask for forgiveness, and forgive yourself for dating unwisely in the past?
- How are you going to explore intimacy with someone in a way that is safe?
- If a relationship doesn't work out, who will support you and remind you that God still cares and you will get through it?
- How can you make sure you are growing deeper with your boy/girlfriend?

CHAPTER SIX:
DATE CLEARER

People always fall in love with the most perfect aspects of each other's personalities. Who wouldn't? Anyone can love the most wonderful parts of another person. But that's not the clever trick. The really clever trick is this: can you accept the flaws? Can you look at your partner's faults and honestly say, 'I can work around that. I can make something out of that.'?
(Elizabeth Gilbert)[18]

A big let-down

Strange as it might sound, falling for someone can be a big let-down.

Have you ever seen someone who has stopped you dead in your tracks and found yourself fantasizing about what they're like? Unsurprisingly, in your head everything is perfect. But equally unsurprisingly, when you get to know them, they can't measure up to this perfection.

Ben fell for a gorgeous girl he'd never spoken to, but from what he could see, she was the funniest, prettiest and cleverest woman he had ever (nearly) met. He dreamed about meeting her and how she would laugh at his jokes, share his interests and be an amazing kisser. Then he got to know her. When he discovered that she was a regular girl with her own sense of humour and interests, he ended it.

Charley fell for a gorgeous worship leader. She planned their wedding day and fantasized about their ministry together and the way he would sing lullabies to their children every night. One day, after the service, she plucked up enough courage to go and introduce herself. They started dating. But when she discovered he was a regular guy who was struggling in his faith as much as she was, she ended it.

Unchecked fantasies, or an inability to see a relationship clearly, can have painful consequences. These stories are extreme (and, sadly, true), but we're all in danger of doing this sort of thing from time to time. We see it happening in the Christian world, where our desire to find the right person plus our strong attraction to someone (especially with the intensity of everyone at church predicting marriage!) means we can end up putting them on a pedestal. And who can blame us? It's a powerful mix! But pedestals are only good for falling off, so when 'God's perfect partner' lets us down, we can feel confused at best and devastated at worst.

We need to come back down to earth. It's time to stop chasing that unattainable guy or girl who will never live up to our expectations (and doesn't exist!). How do we do that? What does God want us to look for? Let's turn that question on its head. What does someone looking for a relationship hope to find in us? What would God want them to find?

Let's get real

Developing clear thinking around dating is a two-way process: we need to see ourselves for who we truly are, as well as understand who we should date (or avoid!). None of us is perfect. The great news is that happiness in relationships isn't dependent on people being perfect! Dating someone who likes us when we are being truly ourselves, and who we like when they are being truly themselves, is not only helpful, but godly. God doesn't ignore the reality of our flaws, but, in loving us as we are, he makes us worthy of love.

If God sees the real us and still loves us and accepts us as we are, let's not fall into the trap of being someone else when we're in a relationship. Being real requires vulnerability, which can feel scary. So it matters that you learn to be real with someone who is willing to do the same.

Holly and Luke fell passionately in love with each other, but as they had both just come out of intense relationships and were about to head off to different universities, they wondered if this was God's way of asking them not to date. On the surface they were happy with that, except they couldn't stop thinking about each other! So they decided to limit the amount of time they spent together, but instead of lessening their feelings, it intensified them.

Holly had put Luke on a pedestal, and regularly told friends that she would never find a man as perfect as him. Luke couldn't go for a moment without thinking about Holly. He was eaten up with jealousy at the thought of her having a good time, just as much as he was being eaten up with longing for her. Eventually, some good friends suggested that maybe they should stop obsessing about each other and go out on a few dates, to see if they were as perfect for each other as they hoped.

So they did. To begin with, it was difficult. Luke wasn't as tuned into Holly's emotional world as she had thought he would be. And Holly had views on things that Luke found surprising. In their own way, they both felt disappointed. But when they got real and chose to accept each other for who they truly were, they began to build a good relationship.

Having the wrong idea about the person we've fallen for can make dating them doubly difficult. Any relationship built on unrealistic expectations will struggle to satisfy. So how do you know whether you should start dating like Holly and Luke, or not date them at all? A good indicator would be to think about how well you already know them. The reason why good friendships often lead to good relationships is because you get to share your real self in a safe environment. If you find yourself regularly pinning your dreams about lasting love on someone you hardly know, ask God to give you the confidence to be yourself and find ways to get to know that person properly.

This is much better, because being a 'blind dater' is a passive attitude that can nurture uncertainty about who to date. If we're going to 'date clearer', our starting point is that we choose to be ourselves. This way of thinking might even prevent us from starting relationships where we're being put on a pedestal that we're likely to fall off. 'Date clearer' also means actively considering who you want to start dating and why. The next four steps of this guideline will empower you in this.

1. Check your blind spots

The unexamined life is not worth living.
(Socrates)

Dating offers us a brilliant opportunity to see ourselves in new ways. Taking a clear look at yourself and your past or current relationships might feel uncomfortable, but it helps you to see things as they really are. Being attracted to someone will always make us act a little as though we're wearing a pair of rose-tinted glasses: we will see things in slightly distorted ways. But there's a difference between being blind to someone's faults in the early days of infatuation and adopting a blinkered approach to *every* new relationship.

You know you're in trouble when you find yourself imagining being married to everyone you talk to! Or you find yourself trying to turn your girl or guy into your 'perfect' ex or that married person you have a crush on. We guys might think we're immune from this, but many imagine themselves going on dates or making out with a gorgeous girl, even before they've ever spoken to her!

The Bible says that falling in love can be like playing with fire, so it matters that we practise seeing clearly, even as our hearts are running wild!

> Don't excite love, don't stir it up,
> until the time is ripe – and you're ready.
> (Song of Solomon 2:7 *The Message*)

So here are some questions to help you identify your blind spots and practise seeing yourself and your relationship clearly:

1. What are you like when you're dating someone?
2. If you have never dated, what are you like around the people you fancy?
3. Do you find it easy to be yourself, or do you find that you become someone else?
4. How would you describe your previous relationships? Intense? Healthy? Bad? Fun? Brief? Stable?
5. Do you drift from one 'unsuitable' relationship to another? Why do you think you do this?
6. Do you find yourself staying longer in a relationship than you should? Why do you think you do this?
7. If you have never dated, do you think you spend too much time trying to change the 'true you' to become what you think people will like? Will that create the potential for an open and honest relationship?
8. Do you have a 'type' when it comes to who you are attracted to? How would you describe it?
9. Do you need to review the 'type' of person you go for all the time?
10. Do you spend so much time checking someone against your 'list of perfection' that you don't give them a chance?

2. Be clear about compatibility

So we're checking our blind spots. Now it's time to work out what we're actually looking for in the person we date. If we're already dating someone, the question becomes: how do we know it's a healthy relationship? The word lots of people use to describe this is 'compatibility'.

Being compatible isn't about being the same, and it isn't just about sexual chemistry either. Compatibility in a relationship means being able to understand each other on a deeper level. There are some people with whom we have an immediate rapport, and there are others we need to work with to discover a deeper connection. True compatibility isn't always immediate, so it's important to enter any relationship knowing that there could be much more beneath the surface attractions that drew you together.

As Christians, we have an added dimension to compatibility in the whole area of spirituality. Dating someone who isn't choosing God's mission for their lives can put a huge strain on a relationship, even if you click on other levels. It's worth thinking carefully before starting a relationship with anyone who is unwilling to explore your faith in Jesus with you. Will this relationship build towards selflessness, faithfulness, permanence and a deepening relationship with God?

We asked a few friends what they look for in someone they date:

> I want to date someone who loves Jesus a lot! Not in a cheesy way, but in a way that leads them on an adventure in their following of Jesus. In a way that leads them to be crazy and irresponsibly generous, in a way that takes them to dangerous places to love those the world would say are unworthy of loving, in a way that causes them to lend their voice to those that the world won't listen to, and in a way that messes up any hope of mediocre living.
> (Jo)

My friends and I used to battle it out for who could snap up the 'hotter' girl. For many years that was all I looked at: a girl's body. I completely missed out on looking at her personality or whether she had a good heart. What I look for now when dating is someone with a great character, somebody who can make me laugh, enjoys the weird things I love and who has an incredible heart.
(Ricky)

I look for absolute honesty at all times. This is the way someone will be the closest person to my heart.
(Agata)

Another misconception about compatibility is that it's only about the good stuff. But what about the annoying habits in someone else you feel able to put up with?

Given that every human being has faults and [this] is endemic to the human condition, deciding whom you are going to marry is just as much about deciding which faults you are willing to live with for the rest of your life.
(Rebbetzin Heller, Jewish writer)

Will you be gracious towards them when they're lazy, because they're still learning how to be selfless? Will you forgive them for not automatically sensing your mood, because once they do know how you feel they're a great listener? Will you put up with them getting over-emotional about small things, because you love their passion for life? But it's OK to have a list of things that you don't feel able to put up with. For me (Rachel), it was a non-existent sense of humour! I once dated a great guy I clicked with, but when it came to humour we were on different pages. In the end, something as silly as him not getting a joke was the trigger for me realizing that knowing myself and what I was looking for were vital in helping me to make clear decisions about something as significant as who I was going to date.

This 'P test' can be a really helpful way of seeing clearly what someone else is about and whether they are right for you to date. It's equally important to consider what this test means for you too!

The P test

What is their/my **purpose** in life?

What are their/my **priorities**, and do they complement the other person's?

What is their/my **potential,** and are they/am I reaching or exploring it?

Are they/am I coming to the relationship as a broken **piece** or as a whole **piece** to make a complete whole?

Why am I attracted to their current **presentation** of who they are (and vice versa)?

Why are they/am I **pursuing** this relationship?

How do my **parents** (friends, etc.) feel about him/her (and vice versa)?

(Devised by Sally Binyman and used with kind permission)

Questions like these can help us get to the heart of the bigger areas of compatibility, but it doesn't diminish the fact that sometimes it's the everyday things that make a relationship work – or not. I (André) once fancied a girl who I was pretty compatible with on the big stuff: we shared a common vision and goals for our lives, and so on. But in practice, we were totally different. Our sense of humour, likes and dislikes, even how we wanted to relax, were poles apart. In the end it was obvious that it wasn't going to work. But some of the best relationships I know are made up of people who don't match up perfectly! We're all different, so let's give ourselves permission to know clearly what's important to us and what we can offer someone in a relationship.

3. Look with love

Compatibility matters, but on its own it's not enough. It needs to be twinned with a clear-headed decision to grow in love with each other. You might think it sounds a bit odd to put the words 'decision' and 'love' in the same sentence. But the truth is that loving someone takes commitment and energy. It doesn't just happen. The relationships we aspire to tend to be defined by people *deciding* to be together, not *sliding* into something they hope will work out OK. Steph was slightly bemused when Charles started showing an interest in her. They couldn't have been more different. Right from the start of their relationship, they realized that this wasn't going to be plain sailing, so they had to decide early on what they were going to consider essential in the compatibility stakes, and what they were going to let go of. They found that their determination to understand and appreciate their differences deepened their love for each other.

Love is defined by God himself as this kind of self-giving gift (1 John 4:8–12). His whole being is a complete picture of true love. It's who he is and what he does. God acts powerfully out of this love: he gave his Son because he loved the world so much (John 3:16). In many ways, God and human beings are pretty incompatible! We are sinners, self-interested mortals, whereas he is the holy, immortal giver of life. But he created us in his image to be in perfect relationship with him. So because of his great love for us, he crossed the divide caused by our rejection of him and brought us home to him. God's love is *always* enough. It's our love that often falls short, which is why Peter encourages believers to commit themselves to seeing one another clearly with God's eyes of love: 'You were cleansed from your sins when you obeyed the truth, so now you must show sincere love to each other as brothers and sisters. Love each other deeply with all your heart (1 Peter 1:22 NLT).

Our attitude to loving whoever we date should be defined by God's love. None of us is a perfect 'lover'! But God teaches us to love unconditionally – even when it might not feel good. We need to handle this wisely, because if our relationship isn't healthy, we shouldn't hold on regardless. Love isn't blind! But if we're thinking of ending a relationship because we don't feel as romantic as we once did, we need to check ourselves. Love isn't a feeling. First and foremost it's a decision. Imagine seeing the person you date as someone you could grow to love in this way. It's a love that is gentle, self-controlled, patient and faithful (1 Corinthians 13). This has to grow steadily over time, as you get to know each other. You don't love-ambush someone on the first date! And when choosing who to date, you're *still* going to be looking for someone you are compatible with. That's good sense. But you're also going to be asking God to teach you how to grow in the kind of love that produces intimacy.

4. Be long-sighted

In this final step, we're *not* saying that your next dating relationship must end in marriage, or even that you should only date someone you can definitely see yourself marrying before you date them. Part of dating is *discovering* whether or not you could get married. The person you marry may not be the next person you date, but if you are choosing clarity in who to date, then it follows that you need to think clearly about the *potential* of marriage as the goal. We have already explored God's expectations for marriage in chapter 3, and we need to keep them in focus as we date. This doesn't devalue a life of singleness, or mean that we shouldn't date more than one person, but it recognizes that we should be active in learning the behaviour that God expects in marriage.

If we pursue people with whom we know we have no hope of forming a long-term, healthy relationship, then we're being short-sighted. God asks us to look a bit further ahead. As painful as this might sound, it means that it's nonsensical for us to continue dating someone who we would definitely never be prepared to marry. Intimate romantic relationships should have the *potential* to evolve into marriage.

So our destination must affect the journey.

If we want to travel down to Portsmouth from London, we don't buy a car and drive via Scotland. So too God's ideas about marriage must affect our ideas about dating. Thinking clearly is about choosing marriage potential in the person we date.

Nathan is a twenty-something Christian and knows that one day he wants to marry a woman who shares his love of Jesus and is compassionate and generous. If he dates a woman he is attracted to but who is also a strong atheist, is spiteful and hoards money, then his relationship will never (and should never) lead to marriage. Not because she is who she is, but because Nathan is clear about who he is and the goal he is heading towards.

Nathan might think it's a bit crazy to limit his dating opportunities like this, until he realizes that having relationships with women who don't have the qualities he is looking for will affect his ability to see clearly. Just like an addiction weakens our self-control and perspective, so too dating against our values will make it harder for us to spot the sort of characteristics we're looking for in someone.

God is more than able to give us all we need in order to live fulfilled lives. We can trust him. If our goal is to be more like him, any intimate relationship we pursue needs to be with someone who is choosing that way too. Christian marriage is a partnership between people committed to serving God together.

There are some ways in which we can begin to see clearly whether someone has what it takes to grow in Christian maturity. None of us will find someone with flawless character (they don't exist!), but it's important to be vigilant for these signs of growing maturity.

1. Are they trustworthy with everyday things, or are they always trying to get away with stuff?

2. Are they able to have friendships, or are their mates just shallow acquaintances?

3. Do they treat strangers with respect and interest, or do they ignore anyone who isn't in their clique?

4. Are they generous with their money, or do they grab everything they can get? (Generous people aren't always rich people; it's about a heart attitude, not a bank balance.)

5. Do they always tell stories where they are the hero/ heroine, or are they able to laugh at themselves?

6. Do they make an effort to get to know you, or is every conversation about them?

7. Do they treat their friends with care, or do they bully them?

8. What do your friends or family think about them?

9. Are they consistent in how they present themselves, or do they show vastly different sides of their personality, depending on who's around?

10. How did they behave in previous romantic relationships? Were they supportive? Unfaithful?

11. How do they talk about previous partners? Being hurt is not the same as being bitter.

12. How do they nurture their own relationship with God and express commitment to him?

13. What has their behaviour towards you been like so far?

14. How do you think someone would answer these questions about you?

We're not looking for the final product, but potential for good growth. That's a relief, because we're still growing too. Sometimes our potential is hard to spot! The 'me' of five years ago will be different from what I am like now. But our good growth does partly depend on being with people who are willing to grow in the same way. Simply hoping that by dating someone you might turn them into a better man or woman is blinkered thinking. But realizing that you can spur each other on to be more than you already are is exciting.

As we think more clearly about dating, we need to be willing to let God develop our potential to be the boy/girlfriend and one day, possibly, husband or wife that God sees we can be.

I see you

There are so many benefits of dating with this kind of clarity.

Imagine saying yes to dating someone who it's OK to be vulnerable with, as you both learn to be your real selves. Imagine if dating them helped you draw closer to God in heart and character. Imagine doing that for them too. Imagine saying yes to dating someone who shares your long-sightedness. Imagine saying yes to dating someone you have a hunch you could fall madly in love with!

With 'yeses' like these, it will make knowing when to say no to dating someone a lot easier.

It'll be easier to resist dating someone unsuitable for you, because you'll remember that you don't need a relationship in order to find fulfilment. It'll be easier to resist feeling 'left on the shelf' if you're single, because you'll know you are already in God's plan, fulfilling his mission for your life. It'll be easier not to feel embarrassed about asking someone out, because you can trust that you're pursuing them for the right reasons. If they turn you down, it'll be easier to resist wallowing in rejection, confident that God will never leave you.

So choose clarity! Don't settle for anything less!

André's word for the guys

Men, we've talked about vulnerability a lot in this chapter – don't freak out!

We can be so bad at being vulnerable, but if we are dating or planning to date, we need to realize that, unless we open ourselves up at some point, we will never be able to achieve the intimacy God designed us to have. It's often challenging to show our true emotions; we can feel the pressure to be the protector, the alpha male, the one she can always rely on. But this doesn't mean we should stop being real. Finding someone we want to fight for and care for means we must be willing to open up and trust them with our fears and draw strength from them. If it's always our girlfriend sharing her heart, the relationship will hit a dead end.

You don't need to be the strong one all the time! Every guy doubts himself at times. But letting your guard down with people you trust means that, over time, it will be easier to handle those doubts. We will have someone who sees everything about us, and still stands by us and loves us. The sooner we realize that, the better and the stronger we will be!

> What I looked for in the woman who is now my wife was someone who would tolerate my fallen state and 'wiring', someone who was prepared to journey with me on that road of discipleship.
> (Arwyn)

Rachel's word for the girls

Learning to be yourself around a guy you like can feel impossible. But remember that you have a unique combination of skills, talents, passions and experiences that make you memorable, intriguing and great to know! Do you ever tell yourself that, once you *feel* confident enough, you will approach a guy you like or start a new relationship? But confidence isn't a feeling; it's a choice. It begins today, with you reminding yourself of the enormous love God has poured into your life. Let him bring out your colours, so that you pursue a dating relationship with a guy who will help you become more of the 'you' God made, rather than a fake 'you' the world around us tells us we need to put on display.

If you are only focused on being what you think a guy wants you to be, you are preventing yourself from seeing clearly whether he is the kind of man with whom you could pursue God's call for your life in dating and marriage. Make sure you don't lose yourself in a relationship, or become so dominating that he is totally absorbed into your world. Knowing who you are, and the call God has on your life, will help you to see clearly who you should date. Remember that, even though there are more girls than guys in our churches, you can still say no to an unsuitable guy!

It's true that guys tend to be attracted to confident girls. We like girls who are confident in their own skin, who we can hang out with, laugh with, be ourselves with. Not girls who constantly put us down, act lairy or think equality is about acting just like blokes. The male ego is very vulnerable; it's just that we don't show it or we protect it in confrontational ways. We need girls to bring us out of ourselves, not to be constantly putting us down. We're looking for a girlfriend who is a friend that we can open up to more than we can to our mates. That's the amazing gift that girls give to us guys. I believe that this is what we're really searching for when we ask you out – a place of intimacy. Unfortunately, sex is the only place of intimacy we see in lad culture, and mostly it's not about intimacy but performance. Without sounding soppy, I think the connection we find with the girl we date and fall in love with is like finding home.
(Andy)

Chat room

- Dating isn't an extended interview or a boot camp; it's meant to be fun. So how can you make sure that whoever you date doesn't feel like they are on trial?
- Who could you chat with to get a wise assessment of your own dating suitability and marriage potential?
- What are the qualities that inspire you and attract you to someone?

- What are the important characteristics that you would want in a husband/wife? And what is less important?
- Read Paul's list of mature characteristics in Galatians 5:22–23 and think about how you could expect to see these in the person you date.
- How could you nurture these in yourself?
- What's important to you when it comes to compatibility? Consider life aims as well as the practical stuff.
- How will you see love more as a decision?
- What part of your own character/views has this chapter stirred you to reassess and work on?
- What annoying habits do you think you have?
- What annoying habits do you think you could put up with in someone else?
- How does/should seeking God first affect you and your relationships?

CHAPTER SEVEN:
DATE
WIDER

Love does not consist of gazing at each other,
but looking outward in the same direction.
(Antoine de Saint-Exupéry)[19]

Happily ever after?

Have you noticed how quick couples are to tell you about the memorable moments of their first few dates? But how often do you hear details of their mundane conversations? How they decide who will pick the other up on the way to church this week or who should pay for the meal this time?

The story of how people got together is always much more exciting than the everyday stuff of making the relationship work, but that's exactly what we'll be focusing on in this chapter: being in a relationship *after* the drama of getting together has faded.

If you've been following our suggestions so far, then you've been considering how to:

- work on your inner strength by getting to know yourself
- make sure you're not moulding your life around finding a boy/girlfriend
- value faithfulness before and during a relationship
- work out if you're ready to be in a romantic relationship with appropriate expectations
- gain some clarity around who you're looking to date and how you'll invest in them

So let's think about what happens after you've started dating. Imagine that you've found someone you're really attracted to and it appears that they're really into you too. Yay! Things are really lining up. You may have been on a few dates, it's obvious you both like each other, and you have had *the* chat, laying out what this new relationship is.

So what happens *now*?

Well, it's obvious, isn't it? You're together: boyfriend and girlfriend . . . but what does this mean?

It's amazing how many people think that finding someone is the only time that requires work! It would be great if, after we had started going out with someone, the relationship just stayed great. Unfortunately, the hard work continues. Some of you who are already in relationships are beginning to realize this. If you want to go the distance with a good relationship, there are some things you need to pay attention to. It would be a shame if we'd learnt to date stronger, deeper and clearer, but then allowed old habits to creep back in again once we found that special someone. It's time to lay some of those foundations that will make dating relationships purposeful, help you keep a healthy perspective on romance and protect you.

One of the best things about a new relationship is that everything is new. You're finding out so much about each other and establishing yourselves as a couple. But with newness comes fragility. Your feelings about each other might be powerful and intense, but your relationship is not very strong yet; it wouldn't take much for things to come undone. As strange as it might sound, nothing stunts a relationship's good growth in the early days quite as effectively as spending too much time together.

Too much time together? But isn't now the perfect time to be in each other's pockets? It's time to tell you about Joel.

Our friend's brother, Joel, is a great lad: talented, funny, loyal, committed to his friends and passionate about growing in discipleship. Heavily involved in his church, leading worship, part of the evangelism team and a volunteer leader of the men's ministry. Sure, he was talented, but more than that, he had rich friendships with people that blessed him.

Then he got a girlfriend.

All of a sudden, if he was not asleep, he was with her. He no longer had time to meet up with his friends. His activity in church reduced to almost nothing. A text from him was a rare event! She became everything to him. Over a matter of a few months, his balanced lifestyle, which had been full of different interests, hobbies and social groups, had evaporated. He had replaced everything that mattered to him with his obsession for one person.

Some of you might be reading this thinking, 'What's the big deal? He's found someone he loves – give them some space.' The problem was that they forgot to give each other any space. This didn't just affect them, but also hurt their friends. It's so easy for this to become the norm.

Relationships that revolve around this intensity of contact end up losing out. Spending too much time alone together creates the perfect breeding ground for insecurities to surface. We all feel a bit anxious in new relationships, because we don't want to mess things up. But rather than helping us deal properly with these feelings, an intense relationship that doesn't involve the input of friends becomes inward-looking. Taken to extremes, people in such relationships can mask their fears of losing the other person by becoming controlling and possessive.

And possessive relationships are unhealthy.

If you find yourself in a relationship where you are constantly fighting, or finding ways to make each other jealous, you need to seriously consider whether this is a relationship you should be in. If you are in a relationship where someone is using their words, fists or emotions to control you, or to stop you leaving them, seek out a good friend you can trust to help you find the courage to end the relationship.

'Hurt people hurt people,' says Rick Warren.[20] Even if our partner is acting possessively because they've been hurt in a previous relationship, we need to remember that we're not fixers. Only God can truly heal people's deep pain and hurt. A girl/boyfriend who won't get help to change their behaviour will never change just because we stay with them.

You may read this and think, 'Hang on a minute! I spend a lot of time with my girl/boyfriend and we don't act like this! I would never hit them or make them jealous.' Good! But the problem is that it's still too easy to put them in the place that's intended for God. By only spending time with each other, we are still creating an atmosphere where our confidence, meaning and purpose come from the person we date, instead of from God. It's an atmosphere that can drain our time, energy and resources, leaving us nothing for anyone else.

The sad reality for many Christian relationships we come across is that they become so narrow that couples lose sight of who they are and cease to live out the mission to which God has called them. If you've waited a long time for a relationship, then it's understandable that you will want to dedicate every waking moment to this new person. But it isn't healthy and it won't fully satisfy.

Live wider

There's a profound fulfilment to be found in sustained intimacy with someone. Nothing builds our confidence like knowing that there is someone who always has your back. But making one person the source of *all* your fulfilment and security is very bad news. 'Dating stronger' showed us that we need a full life, with friends, hobbies and interests, because no single relationship can fulfil us. We can easily forget this when we fall head over heels for someone. Keeping your other friendships and interests alive will enrich the intimacy you are building with your boy/girlfriend:

> The intensity of trying to fulfil all somebody's needs is not something that God asks of us even in marriage.[21]

Just because we are in an exclusive relationship doesn't mean that the rest of our lives are closed to us. Remaining open to God and others is the best way to keep a relationship grounded, godly and growing. Whether or not we ever get married, God asks us to stay connected to the wider world, even when we fall in love.

Esther's legacy

Esther, the only book in the Bible that never mentions God's name, tells the story of how one woman's ability to look beyond her own interests saved a whole ethnic group. Esther was married to King Xerxes, the most powerful man of his time. When his first wife publicly humiliated him by defying his request to stand and be gawked at by him and a bunch of drunken men, he thought nothing of getting rid of her and replacing her with a Jewish girl, Hadassah (better known as Esther). He ruled his palace and nation with fear, insisting that men knew their place as masters and wives knew their place as servants: 'The king . . . sent bulletins to every part of the kingdom, to each province in its own script, to each people in their own language: "Every man is master of his own house; whatever he says, goes"'(Esther 1:21–22 *The Message*).

Once Esther became aware that genocide was about to be inflicted on her people, she approached the king. By law, no-one could approach him without permission, and the punishment for breaking this law was death (Esther 4 – 5). Esther risked her life to save her people. She was a brave woman who managed not to lose sight of the need to act, even though her situation made it almost impossible. In a culture where women were seen as the property of their husbands, Esther's choice to look outward, not inward, is all the more remarkable.

It might be a strange biblical story to choose to make a point about dating, but Esther's story challenges us not to drop our convictions once we get into a relationship with someone. A good test is to ask yourself, 'If I would have spoken out or acted on an issue before I started seeing this person, why am I not getting involved now?' If the well-being of our friends or family is less important to us when we are seeing someone, what does that say about the kind of relationship this might lead to? If, once we are in a relationship, our self-centredness kicks back in and we make everything about just the two of us, what does that say about our commitment to loving everyone as Christ loves us?'

It's a huge challenge!

1. Spend time apart

> Don't smother each other. No one can grow in the shade.
> (Leo Buscaglia)

The first part of this guideline is about spending time away from each other, but spending time apart and being distant in your relationship are not the same thing. Being distant is holding out on someone, which can lead to loneliness, even when you're together. Spending time apart is about maintaining a holistic lifestyle and developing all areas of your life, socially, spiritually and emotionally. It's about living widely and having more of a life to share. It will help you keep a realistic perspective on your relationship. Remember you had a life full of significant friendships before you met this person! You need to value your friends, even when you're dating. It's so easy to make our friends feel as if they take second place when we respond to invitations with: 'I just need to check what (insert name of significant other) is doing first; then I'll get back to you.'

Instead of codependence, where you function like each other's life support (what a mood killer), you are aiming for interdependence, where you each love what the other brings to the relationship. So keep investing in your hobbies, church life and other interests that made you date stronger. Giving each other the freedom to develop is a mark of selflessness.

When Jason and I (Rachel) were dating, Jason started a band that gigged in London pubs. Sometimes late-night rehearsals meant that I didn't get to see him as much as I would have liked. But knowing that my support encouraged him to explore his dreams was great, not just for him, but for me too. It was amazing to me to see how my love for him helped him to grow in confidence.

If you are single, you can be choosing this, and if you're dating, you need to be keeping an eye on this. Even in marriage, it is important to have a wide group of friends who will support you and spur you on. We will always need wider friendships, pursuits and passions to enrich our lives in the way God intended. But it won't just happen; we need to find ways to maintain the balance, no matter what situations we find ourselves in. The idea that we don't need anyone is a crazy one, and certainly not biblical (see Hebrews 10:24–25). The idea that we need *only* one person (husband or wife) to complete us is also nonsense, and not found anywhere in Scripture.

2. Spend time together

If you're dating someone, you need to spend time with them.

That's obvious, so you're probably wondering: what's the catch?

Well, there is no catch. Although we've just been warning of the dangers of living in each other's pockets, a relationship is meant to be enjoyed. You need to spend time together. In the Old Testament we read, 'If a man has recently married, he must not be sent to war or have any other duty laid on him. For one year he is to be free to stay at home and bring happiness to the wife he has married' (Deuteronomy 24:5 NIV).

But before you fall off the face of the planet with your significant other for a year, it's not as simple as that! First, dating is not marriage, so we can't just apply this command to dating. Secondly, it's highly unlikely that a newly married couple would have been sitting around in a romantic bubble, just gazing at each other. It seems to be referring to letting men off some of the duties that would take them away from home for long periods of time, like serving in the army. But the principle behind this command, from which we can learn, is that we should not start an intimate relationship and then not invest time in it.

How many relationships do you know that have started with a bang and then fizzled out after a few weeks or months because the couple didn't spend time together? Jonathan started seeing a girl who told him, 'Babe, I can only see you on Sundays. On Monday I do dance, Tuesday I babysit for a friend, Wednesday . . .' and so on! Although the 'It's not you, it's me; I don't have time to invest in a relationship' line is the oldest excuse in the book, it might also be the wisest thing to say if you know that right now you really don't have the time to invest properly. Being truly selfless, though, means that she should have told him *before* they started dating!

3. Spend time with God

It's inspiring to meet couples who support each other in God's call for their lives. But this only happens because the people involved are seeking God for themselves, as well as together. They're responding to Christ's call to 'take up their cross and follow me' (Mark 8:34). If you're not dating, you have a great opportunity to do this *before* you meet someone, but it's never too late to start if you're in a relationship now.

Spending time with God as a couple and as individuals can feel like a habit that's difficult to get into. If you're like us, you will probably find it hard to maintain. We all have our periods of struggle, but we know that, through it all, God's unchanging desire is to draw us close to him. The Almighty, drawing close to you and me! Making space for this kind of interaction with God should become our priority, not because we're told to do it or we are trying to earn Jesus-points, but because we crave God. Imagine sharing this purity of focus with the person you're dating!

Many people we know find this strange. They tell us that they don't want to pray together, or find it hard to initiate. Justin wrestled for ages over how to get him and his girlfriend praying together. In desperation, he sought out his youth leader: 'How do we start praying? What do I say?' His youth leader paused for a bit, and then said, 'Justin, you simply say, "Let's pray"!' They did, and it transformed their relationship.

So many couples never quite get round to praying and reading the Bible together. What should be a natural activity feels strange. This is where being single brings another advantage. If you can get into the habit now of establishing a good rhythm of prayer, you'll find it easier to keep it going.

If you're in a relationship and don't yet pray together, you can still start. If you make it a barrier, it will be a barrier. Praying is something everyone finds easier to do by doing it. One of you will need to suggest it, and then you will both need the commitment to explore this new and powerful area of your relationship together. In our view, there is nothing more powerful for a couple to do than pray together, for each other and for the people in their lives. Tasha and Joe found that praying together each time they met up really helped them focus on keeping God at the heart of all they got up to, especially when they spent time together on their own.

Sometimes people worry that, if they begin to pray with their boy/girlfriend and then break up, their relationship with God will suffer. But prayer is to build intimacy with God first, not with the person you're dating. And if you don't have a rhythm of prayer outside of your relationship with someone, you don't need to talk to your ex-partner about it, you need to talk to your pastor!

Prayer always leads to action. So think about ways in which you can serve God together. Could you both volunteer together on a project or raise money for a charity you're both passionate about? Could you visit an elderly person you know down your road who doesn't get out much? Give yourselves away together, in the service of others. The only criterion is that it's something you can do together that helps you nurture an outward dimension to your relationship.

> To me, there's nothing more attractive than when I see my girlfriend praying and prophesying after the service, knowing we're doing God's work together.
> (Paul)

> Why would I spend all my time with him?! We would suffocate the relationship. Besides, he needs time to serve at church and home group, and to mentor people.
> (Cerry)

4. Spend time learning

> Give instruction to the wise, and they will become wiser still;
>   teach the righteous and they will gain in learning.
> (Proverbs 9:9 NRSV)

Have you ever heard the old expression: 'There's nowt as funny as folks!'? It's very true. Human beings are the most complicated creatures on the planet. One month we may do something that totally contradicts what we did last month because we've changed our mind or we just feel different. Our moods can alter for no discernible reason. Although we may know what we will be doing for the next few weeks, we can never fully predict our actions or moods from day to day.

So imagine how complicated it gets when two people begin a relationship.

When two people enter into a relationship and begin to share emotions and their lives, things change. Some things become harder; others get easier. Some things get altered, while others become more stable. Being committed to dating wider means recognizing that we need to be humble and open to learning more about ourselves *and* the person we're dating.

After going out with Becca for about eighteen months, I (André) thought I knew everything I needed to know. I thought I knew how to support her, make her laugh, give her space. I truly believed I had it nailed. I also thought that the main way she felt loved was through me spending time with her. One day, when we discussed this in detail with a mutual friend, it surfaced that in fact she mainly felt loved when I helped her with jobs, chores and so on. She preferred it if I helped her with the washing up after dinner, rather than insisting we leave it and spend time just talking or watching TV.

After my ego had healed a bit, I realized that dating someone means constantly wanting to gain wisdom and learning about how to be a better girl/boyfriend. The Becca I date now is different from the one I was dating two years ago, and I'm changing too. Seeking God, growing together and growing as individuals means not being complacent.

These guidelines are here to help you, to give you a sense of direction based on God's desires. This will take work, but we truly believe that, if these are followed, you will feel the benefits of better dating. But we will never be able to say that we have 'achieved perfection'. We could never say that we are 'the perfect disciple in Jesus' eyes'; we are all growing in character. In the same way, we will never be the perfect girlfriend or boyfriend.

We know couples who find themselves unhappy, and break up or get divorced because they had decided to 'coast' through their relationship. What started as a passive and unintentional attitude to their relationship quickly grew into boredom or resentment, as they took each other for granted. We can all be tempted to put in less effort because things are going well or because it's easier not to bother sometimes. All relationships have low points, but love is a choice. We reap what we sow. We choose to love our neighbour every day, so let's choose to love our 'dates' well too.

Gag reel

As the credits roll, some films love to show you all the out-takes captured on location. The gag reels are some of the funniest (or most uncomfortable) moments of the film. They show that, even with a script, a director and an entire crew, things don't always go according to plan.

The same will be true with this guideline. Making space for God, each other, friends, family and wider interests is quite a tall order. There are lots of opportunities for things to go awry and for us to get the wrong balance. But addressing complacency will help us to keep focused on everything it takes to build a godly relationship.

Dating wider is about realizing that relationships don't automatically come with a happily ever after; they're about consistent work and continual learning. Serving God, serving others and serving your special someone is a complicated, invigorating and amazing adventure. There are no two ways about it. So whether you're in a relationship, or preparing for one in the future, guard against complacency, forgive yourself for not being perfect, but be willing to do all you can to build and maintain the relationship. You'll be amazed at how this will widen your capacity for giving love.

Chat room

- What are your interests and hobbies at the moment? What would you like to pursue?
- How do you serve in your church and in the wider community? What would you like to do?
- If you're in a relationship, how could you allow each other more space to get involved in other things?
- If you're single, how do you think being in a relationship would affect your involvement in church commitments, and so on?
- How much time do you make for the person you're dating? Are you happy with this amount of time, or would you like more or less?
- How is your personal spiritual discipline? What could you do this week to strengthen your commitment to pursuing God (e.g. commit to reading a book of the Bible, fast for a day, meet up with someone to pray)?
- How does the thought of praying with your (future) girl/boyfriend make you feel? Why?
- How do you spend your time with your girl/boyfriend?
- Is this beneficial for you, your friends and family? Do you need to rebalance this?
- If you're single, do you think you have time to commit to a relationship at the moment? Why or why not?
- How can you stop yourself being complacent in a relationship?
- Are there couples you admire who you can learn from?
- How are you making sure that as an individual and/or as a couple you are learning and growing in Christ?
- How do/will you 'spend time apart', but avoid jealousy? (See Appendix 2, p. 213.)
- How do you handle arguments? Is this healthy behaviour? (See Appendix 3, p. 217.)

MY DATING GUIDELINES

You've bought the book and read the guidelines.

The question now is: are you ready to buy the T-shirt?

In other words, how do you feel about our four godly guidelines? Are you ready to make them *your* guidelines?

You can tell that we are huge fans of dating done God's way. Which means that, although we think romance is great, our desire is that you build on firm biblical foundations: putting God first, treating others with dignity, being active and intentional in what you do and say, and choosing selflessness. Like the painter with his canvas, these guidelines have been about filling in the gaps based on what has gone before. In seeking to give you robust biblical principles for dating, we trust that, when you face a decision or make a mistake, you will be able to be kind to yourself, assess what happened and try again. So just to recap:

In *date stronger* we encouraged you to date out of a desire to share your full life with someone, not to patch up a broken or unfulfilled life with 'the one', or a so-called 'perfect' relationship.

In *date deeper* we confronted the issues that stop us from choosing commitment from the start. We challenged you to imitate God by being faithful when you date, whether it leads to marriage or not.

In *date clearer* we explored how to go about deciding who we date based on things that can last and that truly matter to us and God, as well as thinking about the kind of 'date' we should be.

In *date wider* we turned our attention to what happens after we start dating. We challenged you to avoid complacency and neglecting God and others as you work at building and growing a healthy relationship.

But there's no point just keeping these guidelines as good ideas if we don't act on them. We firmly believe that putting them into practice will revolutionize your life and the culture around us. Because learning to date stronger, deeper, clearer and wider is not just essential for godly dating, it's also essential for a godly life.

Chat room

At the end of each guideline, we reflected on the implications raised in the chapter, but it's probably worth thinking about dating as a whole too. In his book *Just Sex*,[22] Guy Brandon talks about the importance of knowing what we need to give and to receive for a relationship to be healthy. Use these statements to help you reflect on how you date.

Dating with responsibility

When you're in a dating relationship, you have areas of responsibility, not just to yourself and whoever you're dating, but also to your friends and family and *their* friends and family. Taking on these responsibilities means that you will:

- be honest and truthful to your girl/boyfriend
- treat them with respect in public and in private
- develop your own character, interests and friendships
- not pursue anyone else while you are in a relationship with them
- pray for your girl/boyfriend and your relationship
- give them space to grow
- seek God first in every area of your life

The flip side of taking responsibility in a relationship is that you are also entitled to be on the receiving end of the other person being responsible too:

- you can expect them not to cheat on you
- you can expect a level of openness and honesty from each other, which will grow the longer you are together
- you should treat each other with respect and care
- you should have your own mind and keep up with your passions, interests and wider friendships, and encourage your boy/girlfriend to explore theirs too
- you should spend quality time together, as well as apart

Dating with benefits

When you're in a dating relationship, there are a whole load of benefits for both of you:

- increased confidence from knowing that someone has your back
- sustained emotional intimacy
- a level of physical intimacy that you are both comfortable with and that honours God
- someone to share some of your inner world with
- being trusted and loved
- planning a future together
- being forgiven when you make a mistake
- growing closer to God
- having fun
- enjoying romance

The flip side of enjoying the benefits of dating well is that there must be some no-go areas that both people respect. Every relationship requires boundaries. They are there for either our safety or our success. We could 'break the rules' and overstep the boundaries, but we need to realize that the consequences of doing so will impact on the very things we love about our relationship, such as trust. If you cheat on someone and your partner still takes you back (and they don't have to), you can't expect the same level of openness and trust as before. You will need to earn it again. So, to protect this new relationship, there are things that we know we can't do:

- deliberately flirt with anyone else
- develop an emotional understanding with someone else that you should be developing with your girl/boyfriend
- explore a physically intimate relationship with anyone else
- use any controlling, abusive or violent behaviour
- continue down the path of sexually intimate activity that makes it difficult for one or both of you to walk away
- prevent each other from nurturing your relationship with Jesus
- prevent each other from seeing family or friends
- hold anything your boy/girlfriend has done wrong against them, rather than forgiving it

CHAPTER EIGHT:
SEX
WORKS

*Sex: the thing that takes up the least amount of time
and causes the most amount of trouble.*
(John Barrymore)

Sex ain't wrong

Sex is good.

If you haven't heard that message yet from the Bible, then it's time to start. After all, we wouldn't be here if it wasn't for our parents getting jiggy with it!

Unfortunately, in a lot of our churches the silence around sex has been deafening. The very fact that we struggle to talk about it makes us think it's something God disapproves of. We heard of a Christian couple who didn't have sex for the first year of their marriage, because in their minds sex was such a big sin that they couldn't enjoy it, even in marriage. So here's a chance to explore properly what dating God's way means for our attitude to sex.

Sex appeal

Sex grabs our attention because it's a powerful desire that makes a takeover bid when we're dating – and when we're not! Right from the moment the hypothalamus (the part of the brain that governs sexual reproduction and the biological clock) switches on during puberty, sex becomes a driving force in our lives. Our journey through adolescence brings with it awakening sexual feelings, and every walk down the street can feel like a sexual adventure: 'Does he fancy me?'; 'Does she want me?' We begin to notice one another and the impact a bit of cleavage or muscles in a tight T-shirt can have on other people.

Living in an overly sexualized society doesn't help. Sex is used to sell everything. Why does a bit of naked skin work so effectively, even when we know we're being sold something we don't need? Advertisers call it 'subliminal manipulation'; they know that the prospect of more passion and romance can make us spend like nothing else. But although it can be easily manipulated and misused, our sexuality plays an important, God-given purpose – to help us to relate. Deep within us all lies a hunger for intimacy with another person: to know and to be known.

Dis-ease

From the moment we become aware of our sexual urges, we are also conscious of conflicting messages about how to manage them. Sometimes we make 'just say no' our starting point and hope that putting sex out of our minds will keep it out of our reach. The problem is that this can inadvertently make us fear sex, or God if we have sex, or both. I (Rachel) struggled with this approach when I was dating. When I got married, it took me a while to realize that I was allowed to enjoy God's gift of sexual desire and intimacy.

A different starting point might be: 'I just don't know any more.' This happens when we go too far sexually in a relationship and then embark on a guilt purge: 'I'll never have sex again! I need to end this relationship because it's too much of a temptation for me!' The problem is that we struggle to stick to our resolve. If it happens again, we become more and more resigned to the fact that we're 'bad Christians' or think the whole no-sex-before-marriage thing is irrelevant.

Whether we're virgins or sexually experienced, we're encouraged by an overly sexualized society and an under-communicative church to pursue a view of sex that's unbalanced. We also all suffer from the same 'dis-ease of sin',[23] which results in us being sexually broken. We're not talking about how many of the offences on that infamous 'how-far-is-too-far' list we've committed. That's one of the symptoms, not the cause.

We're talking about our natural inclination as human beings to make everything 'all about me', whether we like it or not. This selfish attitude can be disastrous for relationships as well as our attitude to sex. If we are serious about restoring the balance in our thinking about sex, and our ability to have healthy relationships, then we need to make God our starting point.

So here comes the first big idea of this chapter:

God hates selfish sex.

Selfish sex is greedy. It's all about what *I* want, *my* orgasm, *my* needs met, *my* longings realized, *my* pain soothed. But you don't need to be having sex to have a greedy attitude to it. Dating people based mainly on how they make *you* look or feel, or prioritizing someone's sexual appeal over other qualities, are both symptoms of a consumer attitude to God's incredible gift. Sometimes even asking 'how far is too far?' is selfish, if it's about how much we can get away with, rather than how much we can protect.

Unfortunately, we're all prone to the dis-ease of making ourselves number one. We consume resources and relationships to serve our needs. All the devil has to do is convince us that the gift of sexual desire is now god, and we're in trouble. The Bible calls this 'idolatry'. But there's an antidote. Because of Christ's self-giving life, death and resurrection, it's possible for us to be free from the damage of sin: 'He came to serve, not be served – and then to give away his life in exchange for the many who are held hostage' (Matthew 20:28 *The Message*).

Christ's sacrifice means we can live differently, with our desires in check. The Bible has a concept that describes this way of living. You'll recognize it, but you might never have considered it as a word linked with sex.

It's called 'communion'.[24]

Huh?

We're not talking about bread and wine and romantic dinners here, but recognizing that sex, as God designed sex, means it should be an act of self-giving love. Choosing to see sex God's way means that we value faithfulness and commitment. It's ultimately about putting God first and choosing to glorify him in everything, even our sex lives. It's the very opposite of selfishness. And here's where we'll introduce our second big idea of the chapter.

God loves self-giving sex.

Before anyone jumps to the wrong conclusions, we're not encouraging promiscuity – far from it. Rather than giving ourselves away to anyone who wants us, we seek to put God right in the middle of our thinking about sex. If it is an act of self-giving love, then what will or won't we do in our dating relationships? If it is an act of self-giving love, will we sleep with someone we may be in love with but are not yet committed to in marriage?

As we discover more about God's intentions for sexual intimacy, we can ask him to help us bring our desires and actions in line with his design.

Sex: Bible

You might be reading this and feeling a bit unhappy that we haven't started by saying we should save sex for marriage. We're taking a step back (although we'll be tackling boundaries in the next chapter). That's because the Bible's teaching about sex *isn't* summed up in the phrase: 'Thou shalt not have any sexy-time before marriage.' Thinking that just getting the right 'dos and don'ts' list will help us see sex God's way is missing the point by a mile. It makes out that God is more concerned with our genitalia than with our motives and desires.

Olly and Jenna felt trapped in this kind of thinking. They had been secretly dating for a few months and no-one knew they were struggling. Their sexual attraction to each other was so powerful that they felt totally unable to take control of what was happening. Their relationship broke down in a haze of confusion and guilt, leaving them both convinced that they were failures in God's eyes. Had they talked with people they trusted about their struggles and conducted their relationship more publicly, they would have found it easier to think clearly about setting boundaries and being accountable. Instead, they left the relationship feeling cut up spiritually and emotionally, with warped ideas about God and sex.

We would all agree that sexual abuse, coercion, prostitution, sexual manipulation, rape, using sex to get back at someone else, and pornography are practices that go against everything God stands for. But using your sex appeal to get what you want, persuading someone to surrender their well-thought-through boundaries so that you can get more of what you want, or assuming you have the right to sex in a relationship, are also damaging in God's eyes. For many of us, our dis-ease with our sexuality won't express itself in deliberately hurting someone else. But it might show itself in more complex selfish attitudes and actions that go undetected, or are easier to justify.

Like the Christian boyfriend who persuades his girlfriend to sleep with him to help him stop masturbating over internet porn: *he is demonstrating a warped view of his sexuality that is just about what he wants, and stands against everything God stands for.*

Or the dating couple involved in Christian youth work who regularly sleep together, but keep it a secret from their leaders, who they know will challenge them. They refuse to entertain the thought that this will impact on the young people who look to them as role models: *they are demonstrating a warped view of their sexuality that is just about what they want, and stands against everything God stands for.*

Or the woman who deliberately dresses in such a way that the men in her life give her whatever she wants: *she is demonstrating a warped view of her sexuality that is just about what she wants, and stands against everything God stands for.*

Or the young man who, longing to be sexually pure, tells his girlfriend that, because she is too much of a temptation for him, God has told him to end their relationship in order to seek holiness – and does the same to the next girl that comes along . . .

Or the person who chooses to download albums from artists that glorify violence through music videos depicting virile men abusing their authority over scantily clad women . . .

It's a sobering thought to realize that we may be inadvertently causing damage to people in whom God delights. Wouldn't *he* have something to say about what we're getting up to? Shouldn't *we* have something to say about what we're getting up to? Changing our unbalanced thinking won't happen overnight. It begins by seeing sex as God sees it. So here's a question for you: what do you believe about sex? We ask Christians this question all the time, and their answer is always the same: don't have sex before marriage. Is this what your answer would be too?

You would be wrong!

Well, not wrong in saying that you want to save sex for marriage, but you're wrong in thinking that it's a *belief*. Not having sex before marriage isn't a belief; it's a *practice*. What we do comes out of what we believe. If the practice of Christians is to save sex for marriage, then we need to ask ourselves why.

What do we believe about sex that means we protect it by saving it for marriage?

One flesh

When confronted by angry Pharisees wanting to catch him out, Jesus takes them back to the Creator's plan for sex: that two become one (Matthew 19:4–5). The practice of waiting for marriage before having sex is rooted in the belief that sex unites a couple in a powerful way – physically, emotionally and spiritually. Breaking this bond is damaging (1 Corinthians 6:12–17). That's why we protect ourselves – and each other – by waiting for marriage. If sex is about giving ourselves completely to the one person we're committed to for life, then waiting for them becomes part of our act of loving them.

We are to be tender, loving and compassionate towards each other, just as God is tender, loving and compassionate towards us. We are to be passionate, protective and loyal to each other, just as God is passionate, protective and loyal to us. We are responsible to God for how we use our sexuality, just as we are responsible to God for how we use our time, money and talents. Instead, what we see in society, and sometimes in the church, is that people engage in sex as if it is an act of entitlement and for personal gratification: nothing to do with God. We use the word 'protection' to refer to not getting pregnant or an STI, rather than to avoiding the emotional impact sexual activity might have on someone.

Can you see that being sexual and wanting to have sex is not the issue? Being selfish with our sexuality is.

Selfishness weakens us and limits our vision for sex. Our problem is not that our sexual desires are too strong, but that they're too small. We settle for making sex just physical, instead of everything God intended it to be: intimate, emotional, powerful and uniting. So the next step towards a balanced attitude to sex is to accept who God says we are and to ask him to empower us by his Spirit.

> The problem is that, when the church tells people not to have sex before marriage, it ignores the deeper issues they're facing.
> (Daniel)

You are mine

The main reason Paul gives Christians for not having sex outside of marriage is that we have a new identity. We are one with God. Wherever we go, God goes, and whatever we do, we involve God in it. So it matters what we think and what we do. It's a difficult idea to get our heads round. But for Paul, this idea was so vivid that he told the early Christians, 'Your old sinful self has died, and your new life is kept in Christ with God' (Colossians 3:3 NCV).

> . . . Don't you see that you can't live however you please, squandering what God paid such a high price for? The physical part of you is not some piece of property belonging to the spiritual part of you. God owns the whole works. So let people see God in and through your body.
> (1 Corinthians 6:16–20 *The Message*)

Paul wasn't writing his letter to a bunch of virgins who had grown up in Christian families. The ancient Roman world worshipped many of its idols through cultic prostitution. Pornographic images found on pottery and walls reveal the range of promiscuity people were involved in. Before many of the new converts became Christians, they may well have been involved in orgies and prostitution in temples.

And you thought you were naughty! So Paul is clear to tell them that their new identity as Christ's followers means a complete rethinking about everything, especially sex. For Paul, the only sexual intimacy that *doesn't* fall under the category of sexual immorality is sex between people who are made one flesh by God. In a loving marriage, sex leads to increased intimacy. Outside of marriage, it can lead to alienation and loneliness.

You might not have been sexually intimate with someone because you're waiting for marriage, or you may have already had sex. In one way, it's irrelevant. For Paul, what *is* relevant is the fact that being one with God means you are free to do things differently, whatever your past. Whenever we confess our mistakes to God, we can be assured of his total and utter forgiveness: 'Let us then approach God's throne of grace with confidence, so that we may receive mercy and find grace to help us in our time of need' (Hebrews 4:16 NIV).

It's important to see that a balanced and healthy attitude to sex begins way before you decide what sexual activity you will or won't do when you're dating. It starts with exploring God's purpose for sexuality, appreciating your own sexual appetite and embracing who God says you are. When we are one in Christ, we are no longer bound by our desires; we are no longer slaves to them. But this doesn't mean we aren't tempted.

You might be struggling with sexual sin now or sin committed in the past. Welcome to the club! We're all dis-eased and out of balance. That's why we need God's boundless grace in our lives, and real honesty in our churches.

If you don't know how much longer you and your boy/girlfriend will last without having sex, or if you have already overstepped boundaries . . .

If you're struggling with same-sex attraction, and fear being rejected by God and his people if you dare to say anything . . .

If you're battling with a sexual addiction that is taking over . . .

If you've been hurt by someone who has misused you because of their own sexual brokenness . . .

If you've been selfish in a past relationship and recognize that you didn't honour God or your partner in how you treated them . . .

Receive and experience the amazing grace of the Master, Jesus
Christ, deep, deep within yourselves.
(Philippians 4:23 *The Message*)

We practise saving sex for marriage because we're free to do so
and we want to! Not because we're told to or because we're
afraid of the consequences, but because we recognize the
wisdom of living God's way. Even if we've messed up sexually,
we can still choose to save sexual intimacy for marriage. Knowing
that we're forgiven means that we can set our sights on this
goal again.

Once we get hold of this amazing grace, we can begin to
pave a way for setting balanced and healthy boundaries in our
dating relationship. But before you move on, why not pause and
use John Wesley's Covenant Prayer to voice your own desire to
know God in deeper, more meaningful ways. Only God can free
you from the guilt, despair and sin so many of us feel trapped
in. His great gift of sexual wholeness and hope is available to
us all.

I am no longer my own, but thine.
Put me to what thou wilt, rank me with whom thou wilt.
Put me to doing, put me to suffering.
Let me be employed for thee or laid aside for thee,
exalted for thee or brought low for thee.
Let me be full, let me be empty.
Let me have all things, let me have nothing.
I freely and heartily yield all things to thy pleasure and
    disposal.
And now, O glorious and blessed God, Father, Son and
    Holy Spirit, thou art mine, and I am thine.
So be it.
And the covenant which I have made on earth,
let it be ratified in heaven.
Amen.

Chat room

- What's your response to what you've read in this chapter?
- What do your actions say about your attitude to sex, your current or future boy/girlfriend and God?
- Is God in the picture when it comes to this aspect of your life and identity, or do you shut him out of this topic?
- Who could help you open up this area of your life to God's challenge, healing and freedom?
- When it comes to chatting with your Christian friends or leaders, does accountability go only so far?
- What other things (e.g. music videos, trash magazines, sex talk with friends) will you need to reduce or cut out of your life in order to help you cultivate a godly attitude to sex?
- What questions could someone ask you to probe the heart of your uncertainties or struggles?
- When we embrace romance with no boundaries, sexual desire can easily take over. Have we already decided to keep this in check?
- 'Receive and experience the amazing grace of the Master, Jesus Christ, deep, deep within yourselves' (Philippians 4:23 *The Message*). Meditate on this verse as a way of reminding yourself of the grace and forgiveness God pours into your life.

CHAPTER NINE:
SEX MATTERS

*The church is often called a killjoy for protesting against
sexual license. But the real killing of joy comes with the
grabbing of pleasure. As with credit card usage, the price tag
is hidden at the start, but the physical and emotional debt
incurred will take a long time to pay off.*
(N. T. Wright)[25]

Time out

Tonight you kissed.

The whole evening had been building towards this. Furtive
glances, brushing against each other as you walked. Finally, it
happened. You were both a bit nervous, but it was so good.

So what happens now? A new door has been opened in your
relationship that leads to more kissing, more touching, more
longing. Is that OK? Will you know when it's getting too hot? Is
it different for every couple?

Basically, when it comes to sex, how far is too far?

We probably get asked this more than any other question about sex, because when we're dating we're allowing more intimacy into our relationship. With that comes a deeper longing to express it physically. So in this chapter we are going to address in detail what our relationship with God says about the kind of romantic, affectionate and intimate experiences we should – or shouldn't – have with each other when we're dating.

How far is too far?

> There's more to sex than mere skin on skin. Sex is as much spiritual mystery as physical fact.
> (1 Corinthians 6:16 *The Message*)

Asking 'How far is too far?' starts with the assumption that there are boundaries in relationships that we won't cross outside of marriage. Some people assume there must be a list in heaven of stuff we can get away with before it appears on God's 'they're-doing-it-so-stop-them' radar! There is no such list in heaven or in the Bible, but this doesn't mean we're completely clueless as to where we should draw the line.

Sex matters. If we're in a relationship and not yet ready to make the lifelong commitment of marriage, then the Bible would say that we're not yet ready for the intimacy of sex. Not because it's a killjoy, but because we have already seen that 'sex works' and God is for selfless sex. We might feel ready (in love or turned on), but God's design for sexual intimacy is as an act of utterly selfless giving, appropriate only within a covenant relationship: marriage. So if we want to be physically affectionate and intimate with each other and are not yet married, where do we draw the line?

The line begins in your mind.

You already have a line, even if you haven't recognized it yet. Take a read though this list of the types of physical activity that increase towards sexual intercourse. (By the way, it's not a guide of how to have sex, and we all know there's no set route – but you get the idea!) Where is your line? Where do you think it should be?

Holding hands
Cuddling
Kissing
Prolonged kissing
Touching and stroking over clothes
Touching and stroking under clothes
Stimulating each other with your hands to the point
   of orgasm
Oral sex
Genital penetration

Becca and I (André) have decided to draw our line at kissing. Some people think kissing is too far. But we wanted a level of physical intimacy that was different from what we had with our friends. We've probably all heard advice like 'treat your girlfriend like you would treat a sister', or 'love your boyfriend like you would a brother'. The problem with this is that it assumes that being physically close with your boy/girlfriend is automatically wrong. At the end of the day, it's different when there are romantic feelings involved. Let's be honest, we won't hug our brother or sister in the same way we hug that gorgeous girl or handsome guy we are falling for. We even talk to them in a different way. We felt that it was important to express our feelings for each other. Knowing that we have both set the line at kissing means we're free to enjoy everything up until that point.

I remember thinking around the time Jennie and I got married that [waiting for her] was just about the only gift I could give my wife that the world couldn't also offer. Rings, a fancy dress, a big party, lots of nice food, relatives all gathered around, a saucepan and a trendy electric can opener off the wedding list – it struck me

that all of these things can be purchased or enjoyed countless times in numerous ways. Nothing could match the gift of giving someone your virginity – a proper once-in-a-lifetime gift!
(Jon)

We did things before we got married, but decided we wanted to stop and not do it again until we got married. It was great to know that we could still make that decision, and although it was challenging, it was worth it.
(Aaron)

The other side of the coin is that all of us always have a desire to push the boundaries. The longer you go out, the more difficult it can be. Becca and I have been going out a long time, and our boundaries have been pushed. By God's grace we have never gone further than kissing, but hands have gone dangerously close. We never did look or touch, but we know it is important to rein things in, to go back to our original decision to stick to kissing. Every time we've overstepped this line, we've felt guilty, but this is where we've needed to cling to God and his will, instead of running away and letting our urges take over.

So it's important not only that you draw a line, but that you set it at the right place.

If we conducted a survey of everyone reading this and asked them where they would draw the line, we would find a variety of answers for a number of reasons. Some people might set it where their last relationship got to or where they currently feel comfortable. Others would draw the line at the point where they know they can go and still be in control of themselves. This is the best place to draw the line. When it comes to dating, too many of us slide, rather than decide what will or won't happen. You might not want to go that far again, but once you start sliding, it's really hard to stop.

A word of caution.

There are always two people in a relationship, so where one person feels able to go and still be in control might not work for the other. It can also be too easy to abuse this idea. We can convince ourselves that sleeping in the same bed or getting undressed in front of each other is OK because we can control ourselves not to take things further. But this is playing games with temptation. If we say we want to honour God in our relationship, then we need to respect his desire that we save sexual intimacy for marriage, because sex shouldn't be about our warped attitudes. This means not only knowing where to draw the line, but doing everything in our power to protect that line. Just because we can control ourselves this time doesn't mean it will always be the case. If anything, fighting temptation gets harder, not easier, and control can easily erode over time, and before you know it . . .

Imagine the scenario: you're with someone you love and you both want to express your passionate feelings for each other. You hold hands, cuddle, kiss each other on long walks or while watching a movie. But the moment your hands start wandering and the urge to rip off each other's clothes sets in, the atmosphere changes. Suddenly what has been fine in public needs to be hidden away where no-one will interrupt you. The relationship suddenly takes a secretive turn. When you start to explore each other physically behind closed doors in ways that you wouldn't in public, you're starting to explore that one-flesh mystery.

We know how challenging this sounds, because we know how challenging this is in practice!

This isn't to load on the guilt and make it sound as if sex is dirty if it's behind closed doors. Quite the opposite. Sexual intimacy is a powerful thing that has the potential to unite two people as one flesh. None of us can be sexually pure without the work of God's Spirit in our lives. The line we draw may start in our mind, but the drive to stick to it comes from inviting the Holy Spirit to produce more and more self-control in our lives.

Putting the brakes on

Any line you draw must never replace your openness to God's Spirit when he convicts you: 'God wants you to be holy and to stay away from sexual sins. He wants each of you to learn to control your own body in a way that is holy and honourable' (1 Thessalonians 4:3–4 NCV).

The best way to prevent yourselves from sliding is to decide on your boundaries as a couple, remain open to God, and plan ways to exit the situation if you need to. Don't wait for the other person to leave the room if things get heated. You can take responsibility for yourself. I (Rachel) remember being in a relationship where I went along with anything my Christian boyfriend suggested, because I felt sure that he (being older and wiser than me) must know where the line was drawn. He didn't. It took me a while to wake up to the fact that my sexual purity is my responsibility. With the help of a close friend, I decided that kissing with clothes on was where I needed to draw my line. It was hard, but once I had made that decision, it became easier for us to chat about how we were going to make it work in our relationship.

If one of you is pushing the buttons all the time, while the other one is shouldering the responsibility of protecting the boundaries, you might find this leading to resentment. So find a couple you trust who will ask you the tough questions, and be honest! No-one with a pulse will be surprised that you're struggling to keep your clothes on!

When we were dating, we made a conscious decision not to go away overnight before we were married, so that we would not be tempted. We had close friends to whom we were accountable with this. It meant that our honeymoon was amazing, because we were doing all the firsts together. I just love the fact that it is the one thing we can say we have only experienced with each other. I feel so special that my husband loved me enough to wait

and that we are learning together. As clichéd as it sounds, he
has nothing to compare me with and I have nothing to compare
him with.
(Lesley)

When my girlfriend and I first started going out, we said we
wouldn't kiss. But we ended up hugging for ages and rubbing our
faces together. We realized that allowing these feelings to build
up meant we were more tempted to have sex. When we decided
to kiss, it meant we could be physical in a way that didn't allow
us to go too far.
(Alex)

It's not easy to pursue purity in your relationship, so it's time to
get specific about things. Oral sex and mutual masturbation *is*
sexual activity, so it's wise to draw the line *before* you get there.
Touching the genital areas, even over clothes, will make it really
hard to stop things going further.

You might find that, to begin with, you set such a tight
set of boundaries that you miss out on being physically free
and affectionate with each other. Make sure you keep com-
municating how you are both doing, so that you compensate
in other ways. People whose love language is touch might
need to cuddle on a sofa for a while, not to get sex, but to
communicate love. Similarly, some people might not struggle
so much with not having long sessions snuggling, because
their love language is spending time together or words of
encouragement.

Knowing yourself well, being open to God, and being honest
in your relationship about how you respond to physical intimacy,
will help you stick to your boundaries. Rely first on God's
strength, remembering why you are choosing to set and stick to
godly boundaries. Keep reminding yourself about God's design
for sex, that a selfless attitude to sex works. It will help you to
see the bigger picture.

I didn't think sex would affect my relationship with God, but I was eventually challenged about it. My boyfriend and I decided to stop, and wait until marriage. Sex is so special; I don't want to degrade it any more.

(Tina)

Have a think through these questions:

1. What makes it hard for me to control myself?
2. What makes it hard for my boy/girlfriend to control him/herself?
3. Would it be too tempting to go further if we did this?
4. How do we both feel afterwards?
5. Is it always my boy/girlfriend who reminds us of our boundaries, or am I being proactive in helping us stick to them too?
6. Is this a step on the road to developing a damaging pattern of behaviour that I know I won't like the consequences of?
7. Does this help me to feel closer to God?
8. Can I stop, or am I addicted?
9. Is this in keeping with God's Word and his call on my life?
10. Can I talk to someone about it?
11. How are other people affected?
12. How is this affecting my interaction with other people?
13. Is the whole way I'm approaching our boundaries selfish or generous?
14. Is what you're doing something you would be happy doing in public?
15. Have we started to move down a slippery slope?

What happens if one or both of you have already been down that road with someone else and are now in a new relationship?

Ed and Alice got engaged after a whirlwind romance. They were so well suited, sharing a love of architecture and foreign films. The first year of marriage was great, and then Ed told Alice that he wasn't a virgin. He'd been in a previous serious relationship that he had thought would lead to marriage. Feeling deeply in love, they had slept together, believing they'd be with each other forever. It had broken both their hearts when the relationship ended. A few months later, he learned that his ex had just had an abortion. It devastated him.

Ed never anticipated how Alice might take the news. She didn't take it well at all. It wasn't the virginity thing, but rather that he had kept this part of his life hidden from her as they had planned their marriage. It took a long time for them to be able to rebuild their trust and love of each other.

Whatever our situation, we need to be honest about where we're at. This doesn't mean that anyone is entitled to know everything about us from the get-go, but there needs to be a deepening of trust if the relationship is going to last. Sex can get in the way of that. If either of you have had sex in previous relationships, you need to allow the physical part of this new relationship to develop slowly, keeping the flow of communication open and honest. Slipping into a sexual relationship because it feels like the easiest thing to do will prevent it from growing properly.

> Sex can feel a bit like a trapeze act – exciting, exhilarating, but also risky and exposed! A couple performing on the trapeze need a relationship of absolute trust and stability, and should be prepared to let their act develop over time, making mistakes and learning from them. I'm so glad that, by God's grace, my wife and I were able to save sex for marriage – it's the best forum for that level of openness, danger, occasional setbacks and breathtaking fun!
> (Sam)

. . . Is it a good thing to have sexual relations?

Certainly – but only within a certain context. It's good for a man to have a wife, and for a woman to have a husband. Sexual drives are strong, but marriage is strong enough to contain them and provide for a balanced and fulfilling sexual life in a world of sexual disorder. The marriage bed must be a place of mutuality – the husband seeking to satisfy his wife, the wife seeking to satisfy her husband. Marriage is not a place to 'stand up for your rights.' Marriage is a decision to serve the other, whether in bed or out.

(1 Corinthians 7:1–4 *The Message*)

An honourable life

In this chapter we've encouraged you to decide where you're going to draw the line when it comes to physicality in your relationship. But we'd be wrong if we made you think that all that matters to God is that you don't touch certain bits of each other's bodies! Not stepping over the line is not about avoiding God's damnation, but about aligning yourself with God's design that sex is good, fun and powerful, and should involve marital commitment. Being honourable in this area means laying our desires down and doing God's will. Sexual purity is not simply defined by what we won't do, but by what we will do.

> **honourable** (on-er-uh-buhl) *adj.* 1. possessing or characterized by high principles and remaining consistent to those principles

Chat room for men

God invites us as men to recover respect in the way we treat the women in our lives. Men who embrace a life of honour choose to treat every woman they meet with the utmost respect and compassion. Read through our list of actions and attitudes that a guy will embrace or avoid in order to demonstrate he is a man after God's heart.

When he's single, an honourable guy:	When he's single, an honourable guy avoids:
Explores the life God has given him and invests in other people. Shares his hopes for a relationship with close friends. Asks God to help him be ready to meet someone. Treats everyone with respect. Is accountable to someone about masturbation. Knows there is more to life and being a guy than sex. Serves God.	Obsessing over every new girl he meets. Using porn to try to 'tame' or 'channel' his lust. Thinking that he will easily stop looking at porn once he gets a girlfriend. Believing that not having a girl means he is not a real man. Treating every woman he sees as sexually available or fancying him. Thinking that sex is the most important thing. Rating women's looks with the lads. Adding his name to every rota at work/church, because 'I might meet someone here'.
When he's dating, an honourable guy:	When he's dating, an honourable guy avoids:
Explores the life God has given him and doesn't ditch his friends. Gets someone to pray for him and his girlfriend. Seeks out role models of good relationships that can act as check-in points as his relationship develops. Talks with his girlfriend about sex and how they will wait. Is honest if he is struggling to 'hold back', so that they can support each other. Serves God. Remembers that every relationship is unique. Knows that comparing her with exes or other women is unhelpful.	Any form of bossing, bullying or controlling his girlfriend. Using abusive language to talk to or about his girlfriend. Forgetting about his friends. Telling her 'white lies' to get him off the hook. Using her emotions against her to get what he wants. Only thinking of himself. Talking negatively and complaining about her behind her back. Jumping to conclusions. Expecting his girlfriend to manage or meet his sexual desires. Giving into her sexual desires. Thinking his opinion is more important than hers. Thinking that any problems in the relationship are all because of her emotions.

Chat room for women

When she's single, an honourable woman:	When she's single, an honourable woman avoids:
Explores the life God has given her and invests in other people. Shares her hopes for a relationship with close friends. Asks God to help her be ready to meet someone. Treats herself and everyone with respect. Is accountable to someone about masturbation. Knows there is more to life than sex. Serves God.	Assuming she's not good enough for a relationship. Adding her name to every rota at work/church, because 'I've got nothing better to do with my evenings'. Using masturbation as a way of soothing herself or to generate intimate fantasies around men she knows. Thinking that finding a man is the most important thing. Putting men down. Assuming that she will never find someone.
When she's dating, an honourable woman:	**When she's dating, an honourable woman avoids:**
Explores the life God has given her as she invests in other people. Gets someone to pray for her and her boyfriend. Seeks out role models of good relationships that can act as check-in points as her relationship develops. Talks with her boyfriend about sex and how they will wait. Is honest if she is struggling to 'hold back', so that they can support each other. Serves God. Remembers that every relationship is unique. Knows that comparing a first date with a forty-year wedding anniversary is crazy!	Buying wedding magazines after the first date! Using passive aggression as a way to handle conflict (silent treatment, sulking, etc.). Using emotional blackmail to get what she wants. Assuming the guy is right, just because he's a guy. Dropping good friends. Only being with her boyfriend. Giving in to his sexual urges. Worrying that if he hasn't replied to her text within minutes he must be seeing someone else. Expecting him to initiate and plan every date. She's a creative woman – what would she like to do? She knows he'll love it that she's taken the initiative. Taking all the responsibility for failures in the relationship. Thinking that any problems in the relationship are all his fault!

God invites us as women to treat ourselves and others with love and respect. Choosing to save sex for marriage is an honourable way to live, and frees us from comparisons in relationships that can undermine our confidence.

Chat room for all

- Do you need to/can you make any amends for damage you have caused (even unintentionally) to others in previous relationships?
- Is there someone you respect who is also strong enough to hold you accountable for your sexual attitudes and actions?
- How can you make sure you draw on God's strength rather than on your own will-power alone? What helpful things will stop you giving into temptation?
- You may feel in control of certain behaviours in your relationship, but what might you be doing that make it harder, not easier, to resist the temptation to be sexually active?
- Have you already crossed lines that you had set? Be honest with yourself about how and why this has happened. What might help you revisit the 'list' and set clear and godly boundaries again? What will help you stick to them this time?
- If you're single, what habits have you been putting off addressing because a relationship will 'sort it out instantly'?
- How can you celebrate the appetites you have for love, appreciation and intimacy in healthy ways?

Nurturing your appetite for God is key to addressing your appetite for approval, acceptance and love. So think about how you can spend more time with God, listening to him and soaking up his presence.

CHAPTER TEN:
DATING
DILEMMAS

Over the years we have been asked thousands of questions about dating relationships, so we've condensed them into some of those most frequently asked, and have attempted to answer them as best we can. Enjoy!

1. Can I go out with a non-Christian?

If you've ever asked this question and got the categorical answer 'No', then you might well be feeling a bit hurt or defensive about this issue. After all, no-one would dream of saying you shouldn't have friends or family members who aren't Christians. That would be ludicrous!

For starters, dating a Christian (sadly) doesn't ensure that the relationship is going to honour God, and dating a non-Christian doesn't automatically mean that you are going to walk away from Jesus. But although it might not be a matter of being right or wrong, it *is* a matter of being wise.

The wisest way to date is to find someone who shares your core values and vision. You might love different music, debate mercilessly about which movie to watch, and never really under-stand why they love the outdoors so much, but when it comes to the essentials of identity (being God's child) and destiny (living for him), you need to be on the same page. The reality is that even the most supportive non-Christian boy/girlfriend will have their life moulded by something other than Christ. This doesn't make them a bad person, but it might make them the wrong person for *you* to date.

> Although I love being single right now, one day I would like to get married. But there's no way I'm compromising my adventure with Jesus just to be married.
> (Jo)

There's always the potential that someone who isn't putting God first in their life might accidentally, or purposefully, encourage you not to put God first in yours. This is why Paul encourages the Corinthian Christians to be wise about who they allow them-selves to be teamed up with: 'Don't become partners with those who reject God. How can you make a partnership out of right and wrong? That's not partnership; that's war' (2 Corinthians 6:14–18 *The Message*).

This tension isn't unique to dating a non-Christian; it could refer to anything in life that encourages divided loyalties. But the message is the same: be wise in who you allow to have influence over you. We understand that you may be falling for someone who is not a Christian; it happens. It may even look like you can still be with them and serve God. But if it came to the battle between two sets of values, whose would win out?

Of course, dating *Christians* can present us with distractions if we allow our love for them to take the place of our love for God. Doing Christian stuff (like going to church together) isn't the same as urging each other on in our love for God. We need to approach with caution anything that could split our focus.

If you're currently dating a non-Christian . . .

. . . don't just dump them right away because they're not a Christian! So much damage is done in God's name when we use him as an excuse for ending a relationship badly.

But also, be careful that you don't latch on to any evidence that says it's OK to stay in the relationship.

Some people do date a non-Christian who then becomes a Christian. It's always wonderful to hear these stories, but what do they prove? Someone else's story is not yours. We've seen (and experienced) relationships that have suffered from people not facing up to the facts. Asking someone who *isn't* putting God first in their life to accept that you are is selfish. How selfless is it to date someone who might never fully understand why God will always come first for you? You're inevitably cutting them out of a huge part of your heart and life, and that's before you even talk about your views on sex, marriage and raising children.

We understand how hard the idea sounds that God might not want you to date the non-Christian you're with. So it's natural to feel defensive. Watch that you don't withdraw from your Christian friends because they might challenge you about your relationship. The bond of attachment between two people always becomes stronger when the relationship is under attack (perceived or real), so we always need to ask ourselves whether our desire to protect our relationship is giving us a false illusion of intimacy. We've known couples whose relationships moved from the 'getting to know each other' stage to the 'really serious' stage overnight, because of the criticism they received from family or friends. So if you are dating a non-Christian, give yourself some space to think through these areas:

- Are you able to share with your girl/boyfriend what following Jesus means to you? How do you feel about how they respond?

- Have you been defensive of your relationship? Why might this have happened? Who have you been defending this relationship from?
- Can you pray for your girl/boyfriend? Are you able to pray with them? Why or why not?
- Are you able to see this relationship clearly? Is there someone you trust, who loves you both, who could help you do this?
- Is this relationship healthy in God's eyes? Who could you ask to help you explore this?
- Are you still growing in your relationship with Jesus?
- How might dating someone who doesn't share your focus on God's plan for your life and relationships help or hinder your ability to serve him?
- Would you be willing to end this relationship if you felt that this wasn't the right one for you?
- Following Jesus means putting him first in your heart, so how will your boy/girlfriend who isn't doing this feel about it?

We saw a Facebook status from a young woman that said, 'If a guy isn't chasing God's heart, then I don't want him chasing mine.' It might be easier to say than do, but it demonstrates a clear focus for her life – and focus brings freedom. Knowing her 'yes' is to God's plan for her life will help her to know what and who else to say 'yes' or 'no' to.

In the end the decision of whether we date a non-Christian is about realizing that we need to be wise with the decisions God allows us to make. You need to be prepared for the cost that comes with staying in this kind of relationship or saying no to one, but you can also be reassured that God is more than able to meet all of your needs. Our God keeps his promises. He knows that our loneliness or longing for love can feel so pressing, especially when there aren't many (or any) available Christians on the scene to date. But immersing ourselves in him is the only way to make sure that this fear doesn't dictate our decisions.

Word to the church: We need to wake up to the heartache experienced by many Christian singles who would love to meet someone, but cannot find many people of their age in their churches. Let's meet their radical commitment to Christ by increasing our support of them. We need to be more understanding, place less emphasis on exalting 'couples' and 'activities for families and couples', and realize that, if we encourage Christians to date other Christians, we need to attract more twenty- and thirty-somethings into the church. (Obviously, the priority of evangelism is people coming to know Jesus, not getting hitched, but if it happens, it happens!)

2. Should men always make the first move?

Some Christians recommend that, when it comes to asking someone out, men should initiate and women should respond. But we don't think it's worth worrying about who makes the first move. It's more important to focus on forming a relationship built on mutual respect and selflessness. The less we get wound up about which gender does the asking, the better.

Some guys like to be the one who asks, and some girls like to be the one who is asked. There's nothing wrong with this. We think it is up to you to decide what you would prefer and to act on it. Ladies, if we would prefer a man to approach us, we need to be careful that we don't establish such a strong sisterhood around us at social events that no guy will ever have the courage to approach us, let alone ask us out. And men, if we would prefer to be the one doing the asking, ask! We can't be flirting and sending out 'I-like-you' vibes, if we are not prepared to follow them through.

Asking someone out can feel daunting, whether you're a guy or a girl, but remember that it isn't the same as asking someone to marry you. Skye did it brilliantly; she waited until coffee after the evening service before she approached Jake to ask him out. 'Would you ever like to grab a coffee or go for a walk, just you and me?' she asked. He was bowled over and said yes. She didn't make it into a big deal or get lots of people involved. She just thought that they were suited and then dropped it into a casual conversation.

It's really important that we have a culture in our churches and social groups where people can feel free to ask someone out without unnecessary barriers in place or everyone else marrying them off after the first date! But whoever asks who out, the Bible challenges us to treat each other with selfless love, always being more concerned about their well-being than our own.

3. Does God ever tell you who to marry?

It would be wrong for us to put God into a box and say that he *never* moves in this way. Take Dan, for instance. He was at a prayer night and a girl called Ruth caught his attention. He felt God telling him, 'Dan, this is the woman you're going to marry!' Little did he know that earlier that year at a different prayer meeting Ruth had seen *him* and felt God say to her, 'That's your husband!' About six months later they became good friends, and now they are happily married.

But before you get on your knees to beg God for a similar miraculous intervention, consider the following:

First, we can get it wrong.

No-one is infallible, especially when feelings are involved. Our emotions and longings can cloud what we sense God is saying to us, and we can end up telling God what we want to hear, instead of listening to what he is saying. We also tend to hear these stories only when there's a happy ending, and not the countless others where it didn't work out. When Elisha and Pete met, they both believed God had directly told them, through dreams and words, that he wanted them to date. Things had lined up amazingly, and they began to date and even serve God together. But cracks soon appeared, and after a while the relationship that had seemed so promising at the start fizzled out. Both were left feeling let down by the other and by God. But maybe their attraction for each other and their desire to go out had clouded what they had heard from God? Sometimes our desires can interfere with what we think God is saying. No Christian would ever say they never get it wrong. If you think God has spoken to you, blind faith is not an option!

Secondly, even couples who feel God has given them clear signs still have to work at their relationship.

A word from God didn't smooth the way for Dan and Ruth to happy-ever-after land. God may have helped them to notice each other, but he didn't lift all responsibility from their shoulders. They still had to learn to be selfless, to put each other first and work at strengthening their relationship. They still had to choose to make it work, and not sit back and expect God to give them an easy ride. In our experience, it's rare for God to tell people outright who they should date or marry. And whether or not he does, he still teaches us how to date well and makes us responsible for the decisions we make. We all have to grow in Christ, which leads to maturity.

Finally, everything worth having in this life takes hard work and discipline. Who hasn't doubted whether they've got what it takes to get a degree, succeed at sport, date, get married, even follow Jesus? Often our desire for a word from God is actually our desire for complete and utter certainty, so that we don't need to worry or try hard. For the majority of us, God will guide us by his Spirit in our dating relationships, as we learn, sometimes the hard way, to date well.

4. I think I'm gay. Does God still love me?

Tammy shoved a folded post-it note in my hand. Our seminar was over, but she was desperate for someone to hear her dating dilemma.

It simply read, 'I think I'm gay. I love God. I don't like being different and I don't know what to do.'

It's easy to worry if we feel we're somehow different from other people. The difficulties of thinking you might be gay often feel *even more* complicated when you're a Christian. Will my church still accept me? Will God still have a plan for my life? We might even worry that God hates us for the thoughts and feelings we have. This isn't true, and it's important to remind yourself of this. There are other Christians who know how you feel. Finding people you trust to understand and support you is the first step towards being able to face your feelings and your future with hope and confidence.

Tammy wanted to know two things. Was her sexual orientation a problem in God's eyes, and would she ever be able to have a loving relationship with someone?

Before we look at what the Bible teaches about sexual orientation and same-sex relationships, we want to clear some things up. First, it's wrong for gay Christians to experience condemning reactions from other people in church. Every Christian struggles with stuff; we all need to draw near to God and his grace, and be supported in that. No-one is perfect. Secondly, it's also wrong for gay Christians to feel they are the *only* people in church who are expected to ask big questions about their sexuality. The truth is that all of us need to surrender our sexuality to God. This means that, before we identify ourselves as straight or gay, single or dating, virgins or 'experienced', we recognize that we are God's son or daughter, eternally loved and chosen by him. Putting God first in our lives means allowing him to challenge us about our sexuality and our 'right' to date and get married. The most important question is: 'What is God doing in my life and where is he calling me to serve?' Here's a brief testimony from one of our friends who doesn't struggle with same-sex attraction, but as a single woman has discovered the secret to living a fulfilled life.

I became a Christian when I was nineteen. One of the first things that struck me in my Christian peers was their utter fascination with dating and marriage. It was a major topic of conversation. Not merely fascinated, they were also worried that they hadn't yet met their life's partner. It was an alien context for me. Whereas my secular friendship circle was characterized by a love for life, a desire to become all they could be through further vocational training, and strong friendships across the genders, my Christian peers were narrow in their focus: Who was the one and only? Where could they meet him/her? I am now in my early fifties and single. I haven't received a calling from God to remain single, but so far it has been his plan. He is not withholding anything good from me. I have fantastic work, a rich relational network of colleagues, friends – male and female – and a great church community. What is most important is that his good, pleasing and perfect will is worked out today.
(Marijke Hoek)[26]

Although, *all* Christians should be seeking God's will in their relationship choices, Christians experiencing same-sex attraction are faced with it in a more direct way. Luke's story demonstrates the sheer courage it takes not only to be real about your sexual orientation, but to invite God to speak into it.

I remember, at about age thirteen, realizing that I was different from the other guys at school. As they were becoming increasingly attracted to girls, I wasn't. After a while I started being attracted to guys and came to the conclusion that I was gay. I became so caught up over coming to terms with my sexual orientation that it became the sole focus of all my thoughts and attention. When I started going to church, aged fifteen, I became almost obsessive about it. I begged God every day to make me 'normal' like the other guys. I hated myself and felt really angry against God. It took me a long time to realize that I am more than just my sexuality. When God looks at me, he sees a whole human being who he loves and has created in his image. I don't think of my identity as 'gay'. On the same count I don't think that it's 'Christian' either. My identity is *in Christ* as Luke. That's so much more than either of those labels.

I know God is asking me to be sexually chaste (not have sex), and this includes being single (never getting married). Only he has the authority to ask me this. Even so, it was (and still is) a huge thing to surrender to God, and not even my most trusted friends or mentors could have said it in any way that would have convinced me at the time. I still have painful and dark times, but I am coming to know God and his grace in amazing ways.

One thing I have learned is that, whatever God asks of me, it is still small in comparison to what he can do in and through me as I surrender every part of my life to him. The Holy Spirit can address issues that no human being ever could.

(Luke Aylen)[27]

Although Jesus never talked explicitly about homosexuality or same-sex relationships, he often pointed to God's design for sexual intimacy as being between a man and a woman (Matthew 19:4–5). The marriage relationship is blessed by God and celebrated throughout Scripture, and it is used to explain the kind of relationship he wants to have with us. The focus in Scripture isn't on straight sex being good and gay sex being bad, but that sexual activity that glorifies God is between a loving husband and wife.

Accepting what the Bible teaches doesn't make it easy. One Christian friend told us that he would love to find passages in the Bible that support his desire to be in a relationship with a man. 'But it's just not there, and in the end I can't live in rebellion against the one I love.' It's time that the wider church acknowledged the witness of chaste gay Christians whose lives challenge us to live more radically.

Not all gay Christians choose to remain single and celibate. Some believe that it's not the gender of the people in the relationship that matters to God, but the commitment and love they share. In a way they are right: a heterosexual couple who disrespect and hurt each other don't honour God with their relationship just because they're straight. But it's also not true that gender doesn't matter. The few times that gay sex is mentioned in the Bible, it's never presented in positive terms (e.g. Leviticus 18:22). This has led some people to go as far as to say that you can't be a Christian and experience same-sex attraction, even if you don't act upon it. This isn't a true or helpful idea. Resisting temptation glorifies God. If you have been sexual with someone, it doesn't mean that God will stop loving you, or that you're not a Christian. As with all areas of your life, your choices and actions matter to God. Choosing to do things differently is part of your response to his love for you. He wants you to live in a way that follows him and glorifies him.

In chatting with friends who experience same-sex attraction, we have discovered some things they have found helpful as they decide how to respond to their orientation:

- Just because you've got involved in gay activity (or looked at gay porn), it doesn't necessarily mean you're gay. If you don't think you are, you probably aren't.
- It's important to admit your gay orientation to yourself. Lots of emotional energy is wasted trying to deny the obvious.
- Your sexual orientation is part of your identity, not all of it.
- It's really important to find someone to talk to. It might take a while to find the courage to talk, as well as the right person to talk to. But trying to sort it all out in your own head can end up making you feel more isolated and alone. It's amazing how God can use a trusted friend to help you see yourself as he sees you.
- Jesus fully understands the single life – he's been there and done that! In fact, he lived the fullest life possible, and he never had sex or got married. Singleness is as important to the kingdom of God as marriage is.

- Hang out with people who will help you to remember that God loves you unconditionally and completely. Unless you get your head round this, trying to be celibate becomes about trying to win God's love.
- When you slip up, don't beat yourself up and think that what you've done is worse than anything your straight Christian friend might have done. When God says we are forgiven and free, we are!
- 'As in all other areas of life, true joy and satisfaction are found only in submission to our infinitely loving Lord, who never asks us to do anything that we would not choose for ourselves if we could see the end from the beginning as He sees and discern the glory of His purpose for our lives.'[28]

Whether you agree or disagree with our response, we hope that the one thing you take away is a reminder of God's overwhelming love for you. Whatever your journey looks like, whatever your struggles are, God is walking with you.

If you know that God is asking you not to date for a while, or to remain single for life, you may already have found some great sources of support and friendship. If not, this will be a really important thing to do.[29]

5. People don't approve of my relationship. What should I do?

Often, when people begin to answer this question, they assume that everyone is in the same boat or has the same experience as they have. Our friends might want to protect us from a relationship they see is damaging us, or they might have a few hidden motives! Families will react differently too. We might have Christian parents, non-Christian parents, families who are supportive, distant, controlling, off the wall – anything! As if this didn't make it complicated enough, we all have different expectations of what being someone's friend, brother, sister, son or daughter means.

So it's impossible for us to give you hard and fast rules.

The Bible does make something clear though: we should listen to good advice!

> The way of fools seems right to them,
>> but the wise listen to advice.
>
> (Proverbs 12:15 NIV)

When it comes to our parents, we're taught to honour them (Exodus 20:12). But honouring our parents doesn't mean we have to go along with everything they ask of us. Treating others with honour begins with us doing what God asks of us, and then being humble enough to allow people to challenge us when they think we are getting it wrong. In 1 Samuel we see a close friendship between David and Jonathan. Jonathan's dad is Saul the king, who, feeling threatened because God has anointed David to succeed him, decides to try to kill David. As we read the story, we see Jonathan not always abiding by his father's wishes. In trying to kill David, Saul is going against God's will. So Jonathan defies his dad primarily because he wants to do God's will. Scripture places a massive emphasis on listening to parents, but if it comes to a choice between pleasing our parents and pleasing God, we are encouraged to choose the latter.

So here are some questions to help you think through your own situation:

1. Are your friends/family keen that you grow in your relationship with God? If so, is their advice seeking to help you to do this in your relationship?
2. Even if your family are not Christians, do they often give you good advice/look out for you, or do they try to push their agenda on to you? How accurate or helpful has their advice been in the past?

3. What is your relationship with them like? Is it positive? Unhelpful?

4. If your relationship with your family isn't positive, you might find yourself ignoring potentially good advice. So is there someone who you could share their comments with who would help you to consider the merit of their advice?

5. How will you deal with close friends not liking the person you date?

6. Do you listen to their advice in general? If not, why not? Do you have good reasons not to listen to them?

7. Why are you dating this person? If it's to get back at your family/parents, will it ever be a healthy and selfless relationship? Will it end up causing pain to the people you should be caring for?

8. Do you feel able to continue dating someone if your family disapprove of them? Why does your family disapprove of your girl/boyfriend? Have they ever met or tried to get to know one another?

9. If you've worked through all of the above and still think you're right to be in this relationship, what kind of support will you need?

10. How might you cope if it gets to the point where you need to break some ties with your family due to their unwillingness to accept your girl/boyfriend?

6. Is it OK to use online dating?

I (André) was first asked this question by an old friend. I say 'old', because he was not only a friend from my past, but he was also a fair bit older than me, and looking for love. Some of you reading this have been single for a while. If there's no one eligible to date in church, at work or in your social network, and you don't fancy uprooting your life to check out another area, then how do you meet someone? Why not embrace this modern tool for finding love and join an online dating website? It's not wrong, is it?

No!

Not many things are exempt from God's ability to use for his purposes, and this includes meeting someone online. The real question is: how can online dating be done in a way that honours God? However, before you log on, we would start by saying that online dating is *not really* dating as such. You need to realize that it is more about providing an *introduction*. You can't really develop an intimate relationship with a computer screen! It needs to move to face-to-face encounters for it to have the chance of developing into something significant. So 'online dating' is a first step to meeting someone, not an alternative to dating.

What type of website are you using?

As you probably know, there is a wide range of dating websites. Some exist to bring people together who only want one-night stands. Some just ask surface-level questions and never delve deeper into you as a person. Then there are some that ask dozens of questions that delve into your spiritual life, personality and future hopes, and try to connect you with a suitable partner who shares your vision for life. Some websites do this really well, so we suggest you opt for ones that take seriously your commitment to search for someone who shares your passion for a God-centred life.

Is the way you use online dating sites encouraging you to be a relationship consumer?

It's a hard question to answer, because it's obvious that you want to narrow down your search, and this will include making choices based on someone's appearance and good answers. The problem is that online people-surfing can make it easier for us to forget that no-one is perfect. Keep reminding yourself that a website only shows you people's best bits. The reality might not always be the same as the profile on screen. If you treat it as another way of being *introduced* to someone, then you'll be more likely to put in the work needed to really get to know them. If you notice that online dating is creating a little bubble that bursts easily when the person you're interested in doesn't get back to you, or you discover that they are sharing intimate emails with lots of people they've met online, then it's time to keep a healthy perspective on what online dating is: a way to meet someone. It isn't a short cut to lasting intimacy with someone you've not yet met.

Are you just having online relationships that never go any further?

If we feel nervous around people, online contact can feel more comfortable than meeting in person. It's always easier to meet someone face to face when you know you already have a rapport with them. Messaging, emailing and texting are a good start, but it's important that you meet and get to know the whole person. Keeping your relationship online can create a perfect breeding ground for fantasy to develop, where you fall in love with the person you think they are, rather than who they really are. No advancement in human technology will reduce relationships to emailing and texting. We will always want more, because God made us for real interaction – we need it! So online dating must move to face-to-face dating, otherwise we are just setting ourselves up for failure. The first time you meet up, don't feel the need to plan a whole day; just an hour chatting over coffee could be enough to let you both know if you want to meet up again. And please think about *where* you meet (in public, not at your home or theirs), *when* you meet (when other people are around), *who* else knows (to keep you safe and to be praying for you) and *what* you wear (you want to make a good first impression, but you don't want to make yourself vulnerable). You still don't know this person that well. (You will find some really helpful pointers in keeping safe on and offline at www.christianmingle.com.)

When do you face reality?

One of the great benefits of the internet is that it brings us into contact with more people in a week than our medieval ancestors would have met in a lifetime. But it does open us up to the very real possibility of finding someone great who lives 200 miles away. Obviously you won't know if they can be part of your life for a while, and long-distance relationships can grow into the kind of relationship that you would move city for, but it is a question that must be addressed at some point. It's worth deciding before you sign up what you feel you will be able to cope with.

God's guidelines still apply

Whether we meet someone online or not, the same godly guidelines still apply. If the dynamic of meeting people online is preventing you from dating stronger, deeper, clearer and wider, then it may need to be reassessed. So do reflect on how sticking to these guidelines looks for you, on and offline.

7. How should I end it?

A while ago there was a trend on Twitter called #ThingsPeople SayAfterABreakup. There was a whole range of things that people wrote down: 'We're better off friends' (my translation: 'I'm no longer interested in you'); 'Her: Fine! Him: Fine!!! Her: walks away. Him: walks away. Her: cries. Him: tries real hard not to do the same . . .'; 'We will be friends (Never ever speak again)'; 'Why me . . . what did I do to deserve this?!'; 'I never even liked them anyway'; 'It's not you, it's me!' One honest person wrote, 'I wish things could have been different.' Our personal favourite was: 'I hope you go bald.' But no-one said, 'Breaking up was fun' or 'Breaking up was easy' or 'Neither of us felt upset afterwards.'

It's never easy or fun to end a relationship. We all know that. Yet we still look for that 'magic speech' to end things easily and (if we are brutally honest) in a way that causes us the least pain and awkwardness. But that speech doesn't exist. Even if the feeling is mutual and you both agree that the relationship needs to end, some part of you will feel upset, angry or disappointed.

The Bible doesn't give us a step-by-step way to end a relationship well, but we're *constantly* reminded where our priorities should lie, and it's always about the other person's dignity, their flourishing: 'Do nothing out of selfish ambition or vain conceit. Rather, in humility value others above yourselves' (Philippians 2:3 NIV).

One of the worst lines we ever hear coming out of a Christian's mouth is: 'I just felt like God said I need to end it.' All this does is leave the other person with no closure and a sinking feeling that God doesn't care about them. If God *has* told you something about the relationship that you need to act on, then be honest about it. For example, if you feel challenged by God that you're being fake in your relationship, so you feel you need time on your own to deal with this, tell them the real reason. If you are being selfless and purposeful about the relationship you are in, then you won't come to this decision lightly. Remember that you're not responsible for what the other person says or does in response, but you *are* responsible for what you do and say. They might feel angry that you started dating them in the first place, or disappointed that you don't feel you can stay with them to work through this issue. But those are their responses. Although they are valid, they don't have to change your mind.

Be courageous

If a relationship needs to come to an end, then you must accept that it's going to be awkward for both of you. Your primary objective is to make it less difficult *for them, not for you*. This is what being selfless looks like. Try to respect them as much as possible. Would you like it if someone you love dumped you over the phone, or sent you a text? Of course not. You would want them to tell you to your face, to show you that you are important to them, that the relationship meant something. Doing it face to face is a mark of dignity and respect, because it makes it about their feelings, not yours.

Sometimes relationships are so toxic and damaging that they need to end. You may need to put a bit of distance between you and the other person in order to keep you safe or to stop you from taking them back. In these instances it might be worth getting someone to help or be near by. Being selfless and courageous also means being safe. If you think that your partner may lash out physically or verbally, don't put yourself in harm's way.

Be clear

When a relationship comes to an end, both people need closure. That can mean different things for different people, but it will always mean having a conversation about why it's ending. Some lines to avoid are: 'It isn't you; it's me!'; 'God told me you're getting in the way of my relationship with him!'; and 'You'll find someone better than me!' Use 'I' statements and own your view of what happened, sharing how you feel. They don't need to agree with you, but they need to hear your version of events. This all requires you both to be calm enough to sit down and talk.

Sometimes, after you break up, you can't be friends, or at least not straightaway. Sometimes you need space to be upset and to heal without them being around, confusing you and making it harder to move on. There is no shame in that. Sometimes ending well means not being friends for a while.

Be kind

If you get locked into an argument or a mud-slinging competition, you might feel very tempted (or justified) in saying all kinds of hurtful things to get your own back. This never works. It only causes more damage and pain to the person you once cared for. And this is not honouring to God – so keep your cool and hold your tongue! It doesn't mean that you avoid saying tough things they might not want to hear. But think ahead about what you want to say, so that your words don't run away with you when the anger flares. The chances are that you will bump into them again. You might even have to see them every day! So plan for the long-term and don't burn your bridges now.

Be consistent

Saying something that reduces someone to tears isn't pleasant. Some of us are more likely to crumble when the tears flow. Others might feel OK for the first few weeks, and then all the memories of great times together come flooding back and you wonder if you have made a mistake.

Try not to drag out the ending. Give each other time to talk through your feelings (if you feel able to), but try to avoid endless deep and meaningful chats. It just prolongs the inevitable and can give a false glimmer of hope for you or your ex.

The most important thing is that, if you are the one ending the relationship, you act as selflessly as you can, without going back on your decision. As far as it is within your responsibility, always talk face to face and avoid telling other people you are about to end it. This sort of information has a habit of leaking out.

Sometimes you need to end a relationship because things simply aren't working out. Either way, selflessness is about putting the other person first. If you break up with someone, do it in a way that puts their feelings first, so you know that, although it might be difficult, you have approached it in the best possible way.

Chat room

All of these dilemmas demonstrate just how challenging dating well can be. Even if you've been in a few relationships, there's always more to learn. Look back over the dilemmas and consider what you've learnt or are currently learning about relationships. If you are facing any of the dilemmas we've discussed, how might you respond to our suggestions?

CONCLUSION:
A ROMANCE REVOLUTION

When things get hard, don't look down, look up.
Don't focus on the immediate pain, but the future joy.
(Anon)

A new kind of love story

We guess your head may be spinning by now! We hope that, as you've read this book, you've felt challenged and inspired to embrace an alternative dating culture based on biblical wisdom, and that you've found the tools to make it happen. Now we need to think about what to do next. What happens after we put this book down?

Lots of epic films reach a crucial moment when a rousing speech or an inspiring line helps the characters to face the struggle. There are loads to choose from: William Wallace stirring the Scottish troops with: 'They may take our lives, but they will never take our freedom'. Or faithful butler Alfred challenging Batman with: 'Why do we fall, sir? So that we can learn to pick ourselves up!' Even romantic comedies get a look in, with René Auberjonois in *The Princess Diaries* declaring, 'Courage is not the absence of fear, but rather the judgment that something is more important than fear.' And who could forget Rocky's famous line: 'Until you start believing in yourself, you ain't gonna have a life!'?

We're not equating dating with facing an enemy army or going a few rounds in a boxing ring (thank goodness!), but it's true that, for many of us, our past, present or non-existent romantic relationships can cause us pain. Especially if we are longing to date God's way, mistakes and hurdles in relationships can leave us feeling a bit lost and unsure about how to do things differently next time.

Our prayer throughout this book is that you will draw closer to God and feel encouraged to see how his Word can be applied to dating and your approach not just to romance and relationships, but to your whole life.

God loves dating that is revolutionary.

A revolution will begin when we, as individuals, and as couples, reject the empty love stories of a world centred on individualism, and embrace a new kind of love story built on God's unchanging wisdom for all our relationships. When we live in line with God's design, life makes a lot more sense, and our fulfilment gets a lot easier to find. And the world will have to sit up and take notice.

Where to begin?

First, remember it may be hard to put into practice the changes you're inspired to make. This doesn't absolve us from making plans and setting goals though. Good ideas that aren't implemented help no-one. Relationships are hard work; there's no getting away from that. And you don't need to be in a relationship to get to work on areas of your character or expectations of a relationship.

Secondly, we give you permission to fail! No-one is perfect. We all need to be kind to ourselves and each other as we work on our inclination to be selfish. In fact, accepting that about ourselves and the people we will date is a key point of this book. There is no way we will change overnight, and there's no way we will ever be perfect. Our goal is to grow in maturity in our love for God and others. Someone who can truly say after every date or interaction with someone that they are not what they should be, but they are better than they were, is surely moving in the right direction.

Thirdly, ask God's Spirit for guidance. He is given to us to lead us into all truth, and this includes our relationships. He has the power to transform us: 'And we all, who with unveiled faces contemplate the Lord's glory, are being transformed into his image with ever-increasing glory, which comes from the Lord, who is the Spirit' (2 Corinthians 3:18 NIV).

Where our culture seeks to build relationships on the power of romantic feelings alone, we will build on the rock of faithfulness and commitment.

Where our culture encourages selfishness, we will practise selflessness.

Where our culture says 'the one' will come to you, we will exercise our God-given intellect and take responsibility for our hopes and choices, and be open to his guidance.

Where our culture says feelings can justify anything, we will draw on God's Word before rushing in.

Where our culture says, put yourself first, and if it's meant to be, it'll happen, we will choose to date stronger, deeper, clearer and wider. We will protect our hearts, intent on dating as a way of finding someone we can commit to for life.

Where our culture says that dating their way is great, we say they haven't seen anything yet!

So go for it. Invite that guy out for a coffee. Drop that girl a text saying you'd like to get to know her better. Ask the God of all love to pour into your hearts and minds the courage and wisdom you need to build your pre-marriage relationships on good foundations that lead to fulfilled singleness or fulfilled marriages.

Boy and girl meet,
but in knowing God are already complete.
They date,
and find it's great
to fall and grow in love.
They know the best is never easy,
so they choose to date deep
and keep
minds clear and hearts wide.
They enjoy romance and keep God in mind.
Knowing each is flawed,
they are open, trusting and assured
that they'll support each other through good times
and confusion;
they were happy they committed to the Romance Revolution!
After a while they buy rings and say, 'Yes!'
Dating differently, prepared them for the rest . . .

Appendix 1: Porn scars

*Pornography is harmful because it makes sex trivial,
uninteresting and dull . . . real sexual involvement engages
the whole person in a setting of real life.*
(Lewis Smedes)[30]

If you have ever struggled, or are struggling, with porn, you're
not alone! It needs to be talked about, because it damages our
relationships and the expectations we bring to any new relationship. Online porn use is spiralling out of control. Yet, ironically,
sexually explicit images don't make for better sex or stronger
relationships.

> In the end, porn doesn't whet men's appetites – it turns them off
> the real thing.
> (Naomi Wolf, 'The Porn Myth')

Porn use can quickly become a habit that can lead to an addiction.
The thing that promises us ultimate pleasure slowly causes
horrendous consequences. The extensive research of psych-
ologist Dr William Struthers notes that those who use porn can
find themselves acting in ways they had never planned. He has
observed that heavy porn users become controlling, highly intro-
verted, demonstrate high anxiety and narcissistic tendencies,

have low self-esteem, become depressed and dissociated from reality. We have so many friends, male and female, who say that they want to stop looking at porn, but find it impossible.

When we're addicted, we're not free. Sexual desire is a God-given instinct that is good and should glorify him. Sexual intimacy is something we give, not something we take. Porn turns us into sex consumers and leaves us at the mercy of our craving. It focuses our attention on what we get from other people, not on what we give to them. Although wider society may be quick to dismiss porn as just harmless fun, there is a growing realization of how harmful it can really be.

Porn takes the reason for sex away from God's intention. God designed sex to happen in a committed relationship, which involves two hearts, minds and bodies. Porn reduces sex to nothing more than a *physical* act and drags it away from emotional intimacy. Not only that, but no-one in pornography is married! People sleep with anyone and everyone, so watching it encourages an attitude of unfaithfulness. Psychologists warn that watching a lot of porn can increase our sexual distractedness, which means that we are looking for more opportunities to have sex with strangers. Even people addicted to sex with multiple partners agree that sex is better with someone you love.

Porn places the reason for sex into a self-centred mindset. Instead of sex happening in the context of a loving wife and husband relationship, it happens in degrading, violent or cruel settings. This is a long way from showing the selfless and protective attitude that should go with sex. The mindset of consumerism is also nurtured by porn, because we choose what type of woman/man we want, and when. This can give viewers the belief that they can demand *any* type of sex, such as oral, anal or fetish, when they are having sex with a real person.

Porn teaches untrue 'facts' about sex. Porn makes the sex act too 'perfect' and separates it from real life. Women don't look glamorous all the time, and porn actresses make real women look like attention-seekers if they need long sexual foreplay to help them feel receptive for vaginal penetration. Not all men have huge penises, and no-one can last four hours without a rest! And people don't always want sex, because life is stressful and tiring. Porn teaches us unhelpful myths that will only cause disappointment when it comes to real sex. It robs us of God's desire for sex to be fun and a blessing in the right context. Some Christians even think that watching porn will help them not want to have sex, but this is untrue. Watching sex makes us think about it more, and soon watching will not be enough.

Porn will put us off having real relationships. Watching porn often results in our putting less effort into relationships. Why bother building a relationship with a real person, giving your time and energy, learning to be selfless, which all take hard work, when you can see a naked person at the click of a mouse? Watching porn will also make the real thing boring. Real sex comes with compromise, sensitivity and emotions, and will never match the fantasy in our heads. Porn will rob us of the ability to enjoy a healthy sex life.

Overcoming the enormous allure of pornography is not easy or quick. Just trying not to look at it might work for a while, but then you will probably give in. The answer is to centre your whole life on God. You can be free. You're created to be free. So instead of immersing yourself in sexual images, immerse yourself in God's Word. Seek out someone who can support you as you do this. You probably have friends on the same journey. Here are some resources that will really help you to tackle this issue:

Helpful websites:

http://nakedtruthprayer.com
http://www.xxxchurch.com
http://www.posarc.com

Helpful books:

Stephen Arterburn, *Every Man's Battle: Winning the War on Sexual Temptation One Battle at a Time* (Waterbrook Multnomah, 2009): a Christian approach to staying faithful.

Patrick Carnes, *In the Shadows of the Net: Breaking Free of Compulsive Online Sexual Behavior* (Hazleden, 2007). Patrick Carnes has written a number of books on the subject of sex addiction; this one focuses on internet problems.

Tim Chester, *Captured by a Better Vision: Living Porn-Free* (IVP, 2010). Tim Chester exposes the lies and deceptions of porn, and offers practical and realistic help.

Mark R. Laaser, *Healing the Wounds of Sexual Addiction* (Zondervan, 2004), by a pastor who was sexually addicted and now tries to help others who are.

Crystal Renaud, *Dirty Girls Come Clean* (Moody, 2011), the story of a woman who was addicted to porn.

William M. Struthers, *Wired for Intimacy: How Pornography Hijacks the Male Brain* (IVP, 2009). Christian neuroscientist Professor Struthers unpacks in simple layman's terms what porn does to the brain.

Appendix 2: Handling jealousy

Let's be honest, men and women both experience jealousy from time to time, but they often handle it very differently. In a relationship it can be hard to know what to do when jealousy rears its ugly head. So it's probably worth thinking about how to handle it wisely.

Green-eyed guys

Men, we can suffer from serious jealousy. Often we find it hard to spend time away from our girlfriend and we worry that she might find someone else. Let's face it, we know how gorgeous she is – and how other guys' minds work! Sometimes we think that, by letting her develop her gifts or encouraging her to go on holiday with friends, she might 'outgrow us' and upgrade to someone else. So many men want to control their girlfriends, and might not even realize that they're doing so. But we mustn't let our insecurities smother our girlfriend's time and skills and stop her from growing into the confident woman God has created her to be. We need to let her explore God's calling and put that first.

> When Rachel speaks at events, I know that feedback from me counts, more than feedback from anyone else. It's not just about saying that she did well or looked good (although I've learnt how much it matters that I notice!). It's also about making sure she

knows I'm supporting her and helping her develop her God-given gifts. I want to be that one person she knows she can rely on, but who also points her to God.

(Jason)

If we find ourselves struggling with jealousy, first we need to be open about our insecurities *and* share them with her, rather than trying to control the situation.

Secondly, we must realize that, even though it might feel like it, this relationship isn't the source of our confidence and security.

Thirdly, we cannot use the excuse: 'I trust you; it's the other boys I don't trust' to make her feel bad or get what we want.

Finally, learning to trust her means we have to let go of manipulating who she sees and where she goes.

Jealousy is something we all suffer with from time to time. Being open and honest with our girlfriend when we are feeling threatened and angry is the only way to deal with it in a helpful manner. Easier said than done, I know, but if she's worth it, then we need to be open to changing our natural reaction.

Green-eyed girls

Have you ever felt pangs of jealousy when your man is chatting to a girl you think is prettier or funnier than you? Does your imagination run riot? Do you end up confronting the poor guy with: 'Well, if you like *her* jokes so much, why don't you marry her?!' All women feel jealous from time to time. Those who say they don't are probably living in denial. We feel jealous because we feel insecure or out of control. But nothing kills a friendship or a relationship quite as quickly as jealousy. So what can you do if you find yourself turning green from time to time? Here are some of my suggestions.

First, admit to yourself that you're feeling jealous. If you don't, you'll end up blaming him for something he might not have done. Ask yourself why you feel jealous. Where are your feelings of insecurity or being out of control really coming from?

Secondly, own your emotions. 'When I saw you talking with that woman, it made me feel jealous because . . . ' is very different from 'You're such a boy-tart! I forbid you to talk to women ever again!'

Thirdly, recognize that your deeper feelings of acceptance and security come from your relationship with God, not your relationship with your boyfriend.

Fourthly, have someone other than your boyfriend to chat with regularly about the jealousies you feel. God longs to do the deep work within you of healing your heart and mind, so let him. Find a friend to support you in that.

Finally, develop your own wide life, and encourage your boyfriend to do the same. You will have so much to share with each other and to be involved with together. It will enrich your relationship and stop you from having endless nights on the phone or sofa, chastising your boyfriend for past grievances.

For where jealousy and selfish ambition exist, there will be disorder and every vile practice. But the wisdom from above is first pure, then peaceable, gentle, open to reason, full of mercy and good fruits, impartial and sincere.

(James 3:16–17 ESV)

Appendix 3: Handling arguments

Whether you are someone who puts arguments in relationships down to a passionate nature, or believe that raised voices means the end of the relationship, it's important to evaluate what's really going on. If we don't, we could find ourselves revisiting the same frustrations over and over again, each time with increased anger as unresolved problems resurface.

While it's true that every couple will deal with conflict differently, dating well means being prepared to think about how we can be more gracious, being better communicators, and sometimes asking others to help us get a godly perspective on how things are going in our relationship. Often our frustration or anger can give us narrow vision, and we can't think about anything but winning the battle at all costs. The Bible advises us: 'Don't use your anger as fuel for revenge. And don't stay angry. Don't go to bed angry. Don't give the Devil that kind of foothold in your life' (Ephesians 4:26–27 *The Message*). How can you put this into practice in your dating relationship? Here are some questions to help you unpack how you approach conflict and how you could challenge yourself to react differently in an argument:

- *Do you always need to win the argument?* What might you be losing in the meantime? The respect and support of a friend, or the trust of your girl/ boyfriend?

- *Do you jump to the defensive when your girl/boyfriend questions you?* Instead, could you admit your mistake, or ask them to clarify what they mean?
- *What is your temper like?* Getting angry makes good communication impossible. How could you calm down before you try to resolve the conflict?
- *Are you able to hear what is upsetting or frustrating your girl/ boyfriend?* Stony silence isn't the same as listening. How can you demonstrate with your tone and body language that you are willing to listen?

A word to the guys

We need to watch how we treat our girlfriends in arguments. We get frustrated because she is making things so emotional, but she's probably frustrated that you're not being emotional about something that's important to her! Raising your voice and laying down the law may be what you've learnt, or feel is the right thing to do, but it doesn't resolve the situation. Listening to what she's upset about and repeating it back to her can really calm the situation down and reassure her that you're trying to help. Believe it or not, we don't always need to come up with a solution! Listening is the first step, and sometimes the only step.

A word to the girls

As women, we also need to watch how we treat our boyfriends in arguments. Often guys want to rationalize or fix the situation, and they can struggle with just embarking on yet another emotional conversation. It's not our emotions that are the problem, but using them to guilt-trip our men into backing down is. So be clear with your boyfriend about what is upsetting or frustrating you. Listen to his thoughts and be willing to work it through together. Successfully resolving conflict can really strengthen a relationship.

Notes

1. Pedro Arrupe, *Essential Writings*, Modern Spiritual Masters Series (Orbis, 2004), p. 8.
2. Nigel Pollock, *The Relationships Revolution* (IVP, 1998), p. 118.
3. See http://www.statisticbrain.com/arranged-marriage-statistics (accessed 3 April 2013).
4. Edward Lord Gray, in a letter to John Paston (1454).
5. Michael M. Sheehan, 'Choice of Marriage Partner in the Middle Ages: Development and Mode of Application of a Theory of Marriage', in Carol Neel (ed.), *Medieval Families: Perspectives on Marriage, Household and Children* (University of Toronto Press, 2004), p. 164; cf. pp. 163, 165.
6. Jean Froissart, *Chronicles*, c. 1370: see http://en.wikipedia.org/wiki/Jousting (accessed 13 May 2013).
7. Lawrence Stone, *Road to Divorce: England 1530–1987* (Oxford University Press, 1990), p. 61.
8. Richard Brown, *Society and Economy in Modern Britain 1700–1850* (Routledge, 1991), p. 162.
9. Duncan J. Dormor, *Just Cohabiting? The Church, Sex and Getting Married* (Darton, Longman & Todd, 2004), pp. 74–75.
10. John L. Irwin, *Modern Britain: An Introduction*, 2nd edn (Routledge, 1993), p. 127.
11. Meic Pearse, 'Problem? What Problem? Personhood, Late Modern/Postmodern Rootlessness and Contemporary Identity Crises', *Evangelical Quarterly* 77.1 (2005), 5–11, p. 8.
12. See http://www.pauldunoyer.com/pages/journalism/journalism_item.asp?journalismID=276 (accessed 13 May 2013).

13. Elizabeth Gilbert, *Committed: A Love Story* (Bloomsbury, 2010), p. 79.

14. Zygmunt Bauman, *Liquid Love: On the Frailty of Human Bonds* (Polity Press, 2003), p. 8.

15. Denis Waitley, *Seeds of Greatness* (Pocket Books, 1983), p. 87.

16. Cornel West and Bell Hooks, *Breaking Bread: Insurgent Black Intellectual Life* (South End Press, 1991), p. 55.

17. Visit http://www.powertochange.com (accessed 13 May 2013).

18. Elizabeth Gilbert, *Committed: A Love Story* (Bloomsbury, 2010).

19. Antoine de Saint-Exupéry, *Wind, Sand and Stars,* trans. Lewis Galantière (Harcourt, 1967), p. 215.

20. Rick Warren, HTB Leadership Conference, 2012.

21. Nigel Pollock, *The Relationships Revolution* (IVP, 1998), p. 105.

22. Guy Brandon, *Just Sex: Is It Ever Just Sex?* (IVP, 2009).

23. Rick Warren, HTB Leadership Conference, 2012.

24. We are grateful to Revd Will van der Hart, St Peter's Church, West Harrow, for this insight.

25. N. T. Wright, *After You Believe: Why Christian Character Matters* (HarperOne, 2010), p. 253.

26. Marijke Hoek is co-editor of *Micah's Challenge* and *Carnival Kingdom.*

27. Luke Aylen is founder of Love Regardless, which provides online support for young Christians living with same-sex attraction (http://www.loveregardless.co.uk).

28. Inge S. Anderson, http://glow.cc/isa/options.htm (accessed 13 May 2013).

29. Visit www.loveregardless.co.uk and www.themarinfoundation.org, who offer support for gay Christians. See also www.celibrate.org, providing support for all Christians seeking to live a single and celibate life.

30. Lewis B. Smedes, *Sex for Christians* (Eerdmans, 1994), pp. 35–36.

related titles from IVP

Pure
*Sex and relationships
God's way*
Linda Marshall

ISBN: 978-1-84474-505-0
144 pages, paperback

*'Dear friends, you are foreigners and strangers on this earth.
So I beg you not to surrender to those desires that fight against
you. Always let others see you behaving properly, even though
they may still accuse you of doing wrong. Then on the day of
judgment, they will honour God by telling the good things they
saw you do.'* 1 Peter 2:11–12

Linda Marshall, student worker and this book's author, says,
'Pure *began life a bit accidentally, to be honest, as a six-week
course for young people on what God says about sex and
relationships. It's so exciting to see it moving on to this next
stage where it can be of use to the wider church.'*

'Linda communicates beautifully God's truth and his standard
regarding sex. If you want guidance, honesty and heaps
of grace, this book is for you!'
Beth Redman, author and speaker

also by Rachel Gardner

Rise

*One Life. One Way.
One Master.*
Jason & Rachel Gardner

ISBN: 978-1-84474-504-3
192 pages, paperback

Lively, interactive and gutsy Christian wisdom for teens.

The truth that Christians live by is that the best life possible
is one that's lived in the presence of God: a life that is up
close and personal with the mighty Creator who made
everything. Becoming a Christian isn't just about being saved
from something, but *for* something. The moment you say
'yes' to Jesus, you start out on the greatest adventure of your
life and you discover something utterly priceless: a life lived
side by side with God forever.

Are you ready to *Rise* to that challenge?

*'I love this book. I felt challenged, inspired and provoked –
often on the same page. A must-read for anyone wanting
to go deeper in their faith and understanding.'* Gavin Calver,
National Director, Youth for Christ

'Packed with great insights and illustrations, Rise *brings
the adventure of following Jesus to life in a creative and
compelling way. A MUST-read for any teenager who wants
to walk the talk and challenge those around them to do the
same!'* Pete Wynter, Director, Onelife

Available from your local Christian bookshop or **www.thinkivp.com**

Inter-Varsity Press

For more information about IVP
and our publications visit
www.ivpbooks.com

Get regular updates at **ivpbooks.com/signup**
Find us on **facebook.com/ivpbooks**
Follow us on **twitter.com/ivpbookcentre**

Inter-Varsity Press, a company limited by guarantee registered in England and Wales, number 05202650. Registered
office IVP Bookcentre, Norton Street, Nottingham NG7 3HR, United Kingdom. Registered charity number 1105757.